TATIANA BORSCH

AN ASTROLOGER'S NOTES

Real-life stories on how
the stars shape our lives

Translated by Joanna Dobson

TABLE OF CONTENTS

FOREWORD

Dear friend,

You are reading the English version of my book which was first published in Russian in 2005. This book describes my experiences as an astrologer from the mid 90s to the beginning of the 2000s during which time I lived in my native Republic of Kyrgyzstan (a former Soviet republic located in Central Asia between China and Kazakhstan) and later in Moscow, where I moved to begin work at one of the most popular news holdings of the day.

To put my book in some context, during the period of the Soviet Union, all literature of a religious and mystical nature was banned and came under strict state censorship. Nonetheless, during this period, people published books on astrology independently and studied in unofficial circles and astrology schools. At that time, I graduated from the musical conservatory in piano and was working as a teacher in a boarding school for gifted children and I adored my profession. It was about that time that I bought my first book on astrology and after a while began to study the astrology more seriously. Now it is my profession.

I have always striven to continue learning and to develop my skills and knowledge. Without this approach it is impossible to be a professional astrologer. That aside, the best school for any astrologer is practice. During the period covered in this book, I came across large numbers of people on a daily basis who were turning to me at the most difficult, and sometimes the fateful time of their life.

In turn, I would analyse the stories of my clients' everyday, personal and professional lives, and this greatly enhanced my understanding of life. I share with you here the most striking of those stories that have stayed with me over time.

Happy reading!

Tatiana Borsch

Dedicated to my friends

An Astrologer's Notes

Such is the way of the world that we can never know the exact moment in which our fate might change, perhaps forever. An unexpected meeting, a fleeting glance, a word spoken inadvertently, a modest little book can all turn out to be the first fine stream of a future, which with time will transform into the full-flowing river of fate. Connections we cannot see lead us to one event to another and we say, 'by pure coincidence…' understanding that behind it all there lies a certain force which we can never make fully consciousness. Generally speaking, we prefer not to know our future, perhaps in order to feel more confident in the present and to make the most of the temporal space allotted to us by the heavens. The people who do visit astrologers, clairvoyants or prophets, are like builders who turn to architects in order to build a future home well.

It is not difficult to imagine the conditions the builder find themselves in: dust, a sense of expectation, hope… But what does the other party feel, the person who holds the magic key to that distant future? Maybe this short book about the work of one astrologer will help others to understand the details of this remarkable profession, the only profession in fact that deals with time, and things that have not yet come into being.

I remember my first consultations and clients very well. In fact, I do not think I shall ever forget them. An astrologer's debut is an incredibly complex matter because the task requires knowledge, a high level of responsibility, listening skills, and a certain amount of self-belief. I was lucky (twelve years later, I understand just how lucky), the forecasts I gave proved accurate and my clients were as delighted with the forecasts as I was. It was all quite childlike in a way. I remember one occasion when a woman, who had been fired came to see me and she had a cheery, even outright joyous expression on her face.

"You were right! I was fired two days ago!"

"Oh Lord! What are you so happy about?"

"You told me that I would find a different, much better job and that there I'd meet someone, fall in love and get married. This shows, it's all going to happen!"

My client's confidence in the future was so great that the events of the present seemed so much less significant, less tragic. Fortunately, everything did indeed turn out just as the forecast had scheduled, the new job, the new love and their subsequent marriage.

It was this confidence in the future that gave my client the powerfully positive attitude that continued to inspire her for many years afterwards. Nothing is more frightening than the unknown and uncertainty. These sister-tormentors appear at difficult periods in our lives and not everyone can pass their tough examination, at least not on their own. And whatever the benefit of experimenting with various psychological tools, these can never compare to knowing and understanding what exactly lies ahead. Even the prediction of a difficult period can be meaningful. These time frames are well defined in astrology and clarity is always preferable to uncertainty.

And so it was my very first clients who convinced me that there are advantages to knowing what the future has in store. No knowledge is ever superfluous, not least knowledge of the future. Is there an element of mysticism in all this? I am inclined to think so, for an astrologer really can influence certain moments in the lives of their clients, and the visit itself can become inscribed in the intricate lacework of their fate.

In truth, it is only those people who are 'permitted' to receive information that end up going to see an astrologer in order to receive the information they need to build their lives in accordance with a plan that is conceived somewhere and by something beyond ourselves. If an event is destined to happen, it does not matter who paves the way. It is the result that matters. The story that follows is the perfect illustration of this fact.

SASHA

One day, a strong, fair-haired lad burst into my office with great ceremony carrying a huge bunch of flowers. He was twenty-five years old, worked as a professional driver and had been delivering cars from Germany for the past few years. Philosophy, mysticism and astrology were not his thing but, nonetheless, he regularly read his weekly horoscope in one of the main newspapers and was surprised to find that it was often quite accurate.

So when in the next issue he read, 'in the coming week Gemini's should be wary of strangers because they may not turn out to be exactly who they say they are,' he took the comment seriously. And in fact, he did meet a new client that week, who invited him to work as his personal chauffeur and drive him to a neighbouring city. Having read his horoscope, Sasha[1] (that was the young man's name) turned the job down. He did not think about it too much, despite the fact that they were offering a healthy sum. One of Sasha's colleagues, however, who often went with him to Germany agreed to take the job on instead.

The money passed hands and the wealthy client and hired driver set out on the road together. Before they had got half way, they were chased down by strangers. The client was murdered - he turned out to be a famous swindler who had deceived a group of local bandits — and

---

[1] Shortened, informal version of the name Alexander, most common in Eastern Europe.

the driver was brutally beaten up and confined to a hospital bed for a long time afterwards. Sasha believes that it was the newspaper horoscope that saved him although there was nothing in his individual horoscope to indicate that he might be vulnerable to dangerous circumstances. Perhaps that is why he read the astrologer's warning and stayed at home. That is to say that those who are destined to receive a warning will receive it anyway irrespective of who delivers it and how. This young man became a client of mine. He regularly ordered a yearly astrological forecast and always said that he found them beneficial.

Three years later, when the period of his latest forecast came to an end, he appeared in my office again. As I was too busy to see him then, I asked him to come back in a fortnight. He agreed but five days later something unexpected happened. He lost a large amount of money, which he had taken from selling cars on other people's behalf. The owners were supposed to come and pick up their money a week later and, according to Sasha, these were not the kind of people who were likely to forgive him.

Sasha looked pale and anxious. He had lost weight. He even looked shorter and appeared to have aged overnight. He came to the office and spoke these very words, 'If you had made time to see me, this would never have happened.' It was unfair of him to blame me but his faith in astrology was so sincere and touching that I felt instantly guilty.

As it happens, at the dawn of my astrological practice, feelings of guilt haunted me constantly and were prompted almost on any grounds. I felt responsible literally for all my relatives, acquaintances and clients. And it was not just that. Whenever there was trouble in the city, I felt awkward and guilty. It is difficult to explain why but evidently, when you hold a tool capable of predicting future events you somehow feel responsible when negative events take place, like, 'she could have foreseen this but she overlooked something and so did not warn us'. It is a complex that many beginner astrologers and fortunetellers experience. Sasha asked me, begged me to help him find the thief and this I tried to do.

In astrology, there is a special type of horoscope that can be used to provide an answer to a single question. The chart is structured around the time the question is posed and can illustrate a situation in detail. This is the oldest astrological technique available and was used when clients approached an astrologer without having the slightest idea of the time or even year of their birth. That said, there are still people today who when asked their date of birth answer, 'when the wheat was ripe' or 'when the apple trees were in blossom'.

In days gone by, only very wealthy aristocrats knew the day and time of their birth. So astrologers built charts based on the time of the client's visit and answered specific, practical questions such as, 'Will my ship return from the seas?' or 'Who stole my fish?' This astrological technique is still used today and is very effective.

And so, Sasha asked a very specific question, 'Who stole my money?' The horoscope clearly pointed to his sister and brother-in-law. My client's reaction was sudden and stormy.

"That's impossible! My own sister! Even if she does not love me, she might consider my mother! They'll kill me and my mother will be thrown out of the house! To say nothing of what they might do to my parents! You don't know these people like I do, but my sister does. My mother cries all the time and prays to God because that's all she can do. But my sister, she sees what's going on because she comes to the house every day and her husband is busting a gut trying to find a loan to help me. No! That's not possible! I've always believed you before, but now I don't know what to think!"

It was not easy to take his outburst but I felt for him. I advised him to check up on his sister and her husband since the astrology showed that the husband was planning to take the money and leave. I added, 'the money will turn up and you'll be all right. There's a woman who will help you bring things to light.' It was all clearly visible in the chart.

My client left without saying a word and reappeared two days later. People wear different faces at different times in their life and this time, my client's expression was so strange you might think he had lost his mind with grief. It spoke of amazement, bitterness, suffering, and at the same time an incredible emptiness and lightness. He looked stunned, delighted and at the same time totally spent. It turned out to be quite a wild tale.

When my client returned home, he recounted the details of our session to his friend. His practical friend offered to do one simple thing for him, to place a dictaphone in the sister's house and retrieve it the following day.

"What have you got to lose? If you've trusted this woman, your astrologer, before, then why not trust her this time, too." No sooner was it said than done.

On the first day, neither the sister nor the husband talked about anything significant. It was just the same old chatter about the children, work and other everyday stuff. They decided to carry on the experiment for a second day and this time the results were impressive. When they played the tape, they heard the confident, totally unwavering voice of the sister saying to her husband, 'Nobody suspects anything. You take a portion of the money with you to Germany and I'll take the rest.' This was followed by the description of a detailed plan of how they were going to spend the money and how wonderful it was that everything was working out.

Sasha was not able to confront his sister directly. He was so stunned by what he had heard that he was totally lost for words. His friend spoke for him while my client stood beside him in silence. At first, the sister denied everything and even tried to shame them both for their suspicions. When they played her the recording and it was pointless denying it, she feinted. It was difficult to say whether she was putting it on or not. They quickly brought her back to her senses and demanded the money. Rather than try to wriggle out of it, she produced the larger portion of the cash and told them that her husband had the rest. The husband arrived two hours later and gave them the money without putting up a fight. At that time, two days had passed since the time of the theft.

My client was saved.

"Everything turned out as you said it would but what about the woman who was supposed to help me? No-one like that turned up. I managed by myself. That was the only inaccuracy in the forecast," he said a little later once he had calmed down,

So indeed, who was the woman indicated in the horoscope? It was in fact I, although this did not occur to me at all when I was working on the horoscope. It turned out that visits to see me were inscribed in this young man's fate and played their own positive role in his life.

Once you have analysed all sorts of scenarios, you tend to conclude that every step we take is pre-planned and that we are all dancing to the complex rhythm of a script we did not write. An astrologer or clairvoyant is permitted (if they are in fact permitted) to see a rough plan of the script only, a diagram of sorts, devoid of the tiny, living details. The more talented the forecaster, the more clearly they see the future and the more deeply they understand what is often more important that the forecast itself — the inner world of the individual, which leads that person toward one event or another. The key value of a forecast is the light it sheds on the internal dimension of what is happening. An astrological forecast enables a person to understand the cause of events taking place in their life and helps them navigate their way. We cannot influence what is happening but we can change our attitude towards it and then the situation itself will change. Understanding is often the solution to all kinds of problem.

Events that have already happened are much easier to see than something that is just about to happen. This is something many clairvoyants and astrologers talk about. The former ought to be clear enough as the events of the past are distinctly inscribed in a person's aura and are therefore easy to see whereas the future is blurry. It is not surprising that many clairvoyants can accurately describe events of the past but prove less accurate when describing the future. They find it difficult to indicate time and may get the year wrong, while others might be less accurate when it comes to the characteristics of events themselves.

Some clairvoyants claim that there are many potential versions of the future, while others assert that our fate is strictly predetermined. Neither can be proved. But as someone who has spent many years working with the future, I am inclined to believe that when it comes to most things in life, if not everything, our fate is predetermined by forces from above. There are times in life when a person arrives at a crossroads and they have to make a choice but perhaps, even at times like this, it only appears to the person concerned that they are the ones choosing.

Great prophets and famous clairvoyants alike claim that the past, present and future exist simultaneously, and, therefore, you can talk about the future in the same way as you can talk about the past. If this is so, then our destiny must be predetermined and unchangeable.

Sometimes, astrologers come across cases in which it appears that a person has not achieved their full potential or has let opportunities pass them by. This often happens when, in order to take a step forward in life, something familiar must be left behind, as they say, 'jumping into the void empty-handed'. These lost opportunities are visible in a person's horoscope, and anyway, people usually have a clear sense of them.

'If only I had been a bit bolder!' they say. But there are no 'if only' passes in life. The past cannot be redone or returned.

Astrologers are not clairvoyants but they have a powerful tool at their disposal that has been honed over thousands of years. Astrology is more structured than clairvoyance. There are clear principles that prevent the astrologer from going astray, once they know how to apply them. In addition, all practicing astrologers have the gift of foresight. You might think that if there are principles and mathematical calculations at work, it would not make any difference whether an astrologer were analysing the past or the future. However, there is a difference and the past reads much more easily than the future.

In predicting the future, you always have to overcome the invisible obstacle of time. Time is capricious. It has the tendency to resist and will only let in the most fanatical and persistent.

Astrology is in fact a profession for fanatics. It is like a disease that, once it has taken hold of you, never lets go. It starts like a genuine illness with acute attacks, sleepless nights and fevers. I am sure that anyone who has practiced astrology will know what I am talking about. It leaves no time for anything else and, like a demanding wife, won't stand for competition. People will abandon their former activities and profession and completely change their lives for the sake of astrology. This happened to me once just as it has to many professional astrologers.

The day I bought my first astrology book, I had no idea that it would change my life. With a wonderful profession that I loved, how could I have imagined that three years later, I would leave it all behind?

As a professional pianist, I had taken the long path to being a classical musician: school, college, the conservatory. I had a wonderful class, much loved students and aside from that, I found great pleasure in working with rhythmic gymnasts.

However, astrology turned out to be the stronger pull and although I tried very hard to combine my passion for this newfound art with my career in music, I was quickly put in my place. I clearly remember the day when my favourite student came to tell me that she was leaving.

"You're not interested in music any more. You've changed. You're completely different now. And for that reason, I'm leaving." It was true. This fine, intuitive, talented individual, a fourteen-year-old girl, was the first to sense the changes taking place inside me. Other students followed her example.

I understood perfectly what was happening. On an energetic level, I had left music a long time before but had been too afraid to take the first step into what felt like nowhere. But change was essential and I was literally squeezed out of what was already obsolete in my life without any care for my opinion on the matter.

And so my new life began and at first, no-one approved or understood. Only later, when astrology started to become popular did people begin to change their attitude toward me. This is not something that is unique to my path. Not so long ago, I heard a similar story from a good friend, a famous and very well-established astrologer. She used to be a successful banker but then became interested in astrology and gave everything up to do what she loved.

Astrology is not something that can be learned for the sake of earning one's bread and butter. This she will not forgive. For this reason, it tends to be the case that established astrologers have experience of a successful career in a different field and came to astrology because they could not do otherwise. Astrology is like a bottomless well. People devote their lives to its study and yet are always tormented by doubt over whether they are a true professional or just so-so. Astrology is something that cannot be studied without love for the subject, for it is only love that is strong enough to overcome the obstacles that the beginner astrologer inevitably encounters. And the obstacles are many. In addition to a good professional grounding, working as an astrologer requires having a strong sense of one's own inner values, the ability to communicate with people and understand them even when doing so seems impossible. The person sitting opposite you could be anyone in the eyes of others, a genius, a criminal, a hero, but for you they are a person, like any other, who is asking for your help.

The astrologer evaluates events in a very different way to their client. The astrologer's task is to help a person understand why they have ended up in any given situation. Sooner or later, there comes a time in every person's life when they ask themselves the question, 'why am I here, and why is this happening to me?' and it is in search of the answers that people find themselves turning to an astrologer.

Can an astrologer help anyone and everyone? Unfortunately not. Some people can be helped, others it seems are not destined to be helped. Every astrologer eventually forms a circle of regular clients, people who are able to work with the information the astrologer communicates to them. The ability to listen and to hear (and these are quite different things) is the main characteristic of people who benefit from astrology just as the ability to correctly, tactfully and carefully convey information is the main quality of any experienced, talented astrologer. The mutual communication that takes place between astrologer and client changes and enriches both parties. This, of course, is the ideal but still, it is not uncommon in astrological practice. What could compare to being able to reveal to a person their best qualities and potential and in this way make their lives richer and happier?

I remember a case in which the story of Cinderella came to life in a curious way with the help of astrology.

CINDERELLA

Cinderella had just turned 40 and she was very lonely. As befits the character of Cinderella, she was very hardworking and had never married. She was untidy and unattractive, overweight, had a mealy complexion and clearly put no thought into how she dressed. When I first saw her, she was wearing a strange hat with pink flowers, a bright colourful dress and white sandals with visibly worn down heels. She looked much older than 40. At the same time, there was something about her, you could say an almost childlike naivety, a purity, a certain decency and aura of goodwill. She had a kind, open face, a pleasant smile, and appeared to have a timid, delicate and trusting manner. It was almost as if the exceptionally considerate, open-hearted soul, which shone out through the blue eyes and timid smile had been mistakenly placed inside this awkward body. Naturally, it worried my client that she was still alone at her age and she wondered whether she had any chance at all of ever meeting Mr. Right.

Having cast her horoscope, I was delighted to see that she would get married and quite soon at that, in eighteen months to two years from now. Her husband would be someone of a different nationality and after getting married she would leave Russia forever.

It is always a pleasure to give an optimistic prediction! I looked at my client carefully and even doubted the verity of my own conclusions so little did they seem to fit with her untidy appearance. I checked the chart again and then told the woman how I saw her future. She was not at all surprised and, in turn, said that she had long been thinking of getting in contact with a dating agency that worked with foreign clients but had been too shy to do so.

"Now I'll go for sure!" she solemnly stated. "I so needed some support and now I have it."

It should be said that many people anticipate their own future and seem to turn to an astrologer looking for confirmation of their own plans and intentions. 'That's just what I thought!', 'You've confirmed what I suspected!' I often hear these words after a consultation. And it is not surprising really because the future lives within us. It is the unfolding of a certain personal program and if you are close to your centre and heed the inner voice, you can predict many events relating to the near and the more distant future.

Unfortunately, however, very few people are able to listen to the soul and to hear what it is trying to tell them. It requires a person to step back from the constant flow of external events, meetings and people and devote time to oneself in solitude.

What is also surprising is that although almost everyone looks after their external appearance, (the empire of the beauty industry is built on our need to look good) very few have the time or the desire to put their inner world in order. And yet there is not a hairdresser, cosmetologist, fashion designer or plastic surgeon in the world, who can give a person that thing called charm. Charm is a characteristic of those who perfect not only their outer appearance but their inner world, too. Emotionally sensitive, clever people who have lived a lot and thought a lot are always charming. The same can be said of inner integrity and purity. These qualities too are always charming.

And so, my visitor left and I did not see her for about a year. Then, one day, the owner of the dating agency came to see me.

"Who is this woman you sent us?" she asked with a tone of irony. "You surely don't believe that this woman could ever marry a foreigner? There are really beautiful women who can't find a partner, but her..." and then she waved her hand cynically. "I suppose it never harmed anyone to dream, especially with the help of an astrologer."

"Pretty is as pretty does," I replied. And then exactly one year after her first visit my client reappeared. She seemed scared, confused and embarrassed.

"I've started corresponding with a man from Germany, and now he's invited me to visit. I'm terrified that he won't like me. I mean, I'm fat, ugly and middle-aged. Maybe I should forget about it and just not go. I could still write to him and he would reply. Even that is a rare thing for me. But if I go and he's disappointed I won't have love or letters or hope."

"But you've sent him photographs of yourself, right?"

"Yes but only a portrait photo. They did an artistic touchup so it doesn't look anything like me in real life. What do you think I should do? I have complete trust in you."

'I have complete trust in you...' This seemingly simple phrase can have a rather strange effect on a person. When an individual says something like this, they are putting you on a pedestal at the same time as handing over full responsibility for what is going to happen next. Naturally there is no way you can say, 'but you really shouldn't trust me' otherwise why would you be working as an astrologer in the first place? And getting into long explanations about how an astrologer and God are different things is not quite the appropriate thing to do in a moment like this either. The best thing I could do was to draw up her chart, which is what I did. To my joy, when I read the chart I could see that she would travel to Germany and there her ships would come in.

"Really? Is that really possible? You aren't just saying that because you feel sorry for me? You're actually saying that he might like me? Really?" Her reaction was so passionate that I understood the situation. She was in love with this man and his letters and what he might be like in reality did not seem to concern her at all. At least, she did not ask me a single question about the man she had not yet met, which could only mean one thing - he was a good person and this was no time for doubt.

So, having taken the first step towards her fate (by contacting an astrologer and joining a dating agency), my client now had to take the second step by going on this trip and meeting her beloved in person. I chose the most successful time for the trip and she left much calmer than when she had arrived. I asked her to pop in or to call me and let me know how the trip had gone.

It should be said that once you start working with a client's horoscope, you involuntarily become, if not a friend, then certainly a kind of confidant. A client might tell you things they have never told another and this kind of trust always establishes a mutual relationship. A client may rely on you, your experience and knowledge but you have to firmly and kindly nip things in the bud if a client starts to raise you to the ranks of messiah, which many clients have the tendency to do. Playing God is a dangerous game for both parties, for the client and for the astrologer (or clairvoyant). It always ends in pain and disappointment.

The statements of many sorcerers and clairvoyants, that they can change a person's karma, correct their fate and make a lover appear or disappear, ought to evoke disgust and distrust in any normal person. If such people do exist, then what would be the point of our lives? What would be the point of doing anything, of working and striving when you can just pay a sorcerer and be happy? Really, I mean why endure pain and suffering if there is a short cut to happiness? It is the desire for quick and easy happiness that leads people to the sorcerer, who longs to sit on the throne instead of God for a while so that they can decide what is right and what is wrong in life. When a person believes that their fate lies in the hands of the sorcerer, they give that individual huge power over them.

Having dealings with unscrupulous individuals who claim to be able to predict, 'cast spells' and 'bewitch' is also extremely dangerous, since at best, the 'client' will suffer material losses, and at worst, the whole thing will lead to serious psychological trauma.

I remember a case in which a woman deftly manipulated her wealthy husband via an old acquaintance, a fortuneteller. At the point at which he started believing the fortuneteller's predictions, they had him, hook, line and sinker. After that, the wife used the fortuneteller whenever she wanted to 'remove' from their lives anyone she found objectionable. Small-minded and far from attractive, she was afraid of losing influence over her husband and so surrounded herself with people who were loyal to her above her husband.

It was not long before the gullible husband found himself at the centre of a gaping void. He stopped spending time with the people he truly respected and to whom he felt a genuine connection. The set-up was simple: every time the wife required someone to be 'distanced', she did a deal with the fortuneteller, who informed her client of what was allegedly 'going on' in his inner circle. Many important bonds were severed as a result and the man became distrustful and suspicious.

Fortunately, there is a huge difference between a professional astrologer and those who claim to be able to play the role of God in other people's lives. Astrologers know the limits of their authority very well and would never promise 'butter mountains and wine lakes'. Nor would they ever interfere in the private life of another for purely selfish interests.

An astrologer forecasts a situation and helps the client find their way within in. In addition, an astrologer may act as a psychologist, since the explanation of one problem or another often requires certain psychological skills as well as life experience. A certain famous astrologer once very rightly remarked, 'An experienced astrologer must not only have an excellent knowledge of astrology; They must have excellent knowledge of life.'

In Russia, very few people use psychologists; in our country, the profession does not have the same appeal as is does in the West. This might be because talking with friends around the kitchen table over a cup of coffee or something stronger partly replaces the conversations one might have with a psychologist. If something happens, we turn first to a girlfriend or other close friend. This custom does not exist in quite the same way in the West, where people do not tend to talk about their problems and where the psychologist may be a person's only confidant. Psychology, such as it exists in Russia can sometimes cause more problems than it solves.

The advantage of astro-psychology is that, along with psychoanalysis side of things, it provides a forecast that gives a clear structure to a person's life — a kind of vector that in itself can solve many psychological problems.

But let us return to our client. Her trip was surprisingly successful. As she alighted the train, she was greeted by a cheerful, handsome man. Shy and embarrassed, she started apologising for being fat. He simply said, 'Being overweight is like being ill. If you move out here, we will cure you.'

After her three-week stay in Germany, my client was changed beyond recognition. She lost a little weight and began to dress differently. Her fiancé - by this time he was her fiancé! - dressed her to his taste and it really suited her. But most importantly, her eyes shone with love and she never stopped smiling. She was a living embodiment of light, joy and love. And God knows, she was beautiful! Six months later, the groom claimed her as his own forever. I have to say, many were surprised by this story especially the women from the dating agency. One of the first to marry was their least promising client whom they had instantly given up as a bad job.

Half-jokingly, half-seriously, the owner of the bureau once said to me, 'that was your doing. You must have put a spell on her husband'. After this incident, a whole queue of beautiful young woman came to me, all dreaming of finding a suitor overseas.

It has to be said that neither appearance, age nor education are the key to a successful marriage. Position, status, age, character, and the nationality of one's future partner can all be seen in the natal chart, defined as they are at the moment of birth, or perhaps even earlier, no doubt much earlier. That is to say that the seeds of our successes and our troubles are rooted in our past lives. This explains the distribution of life's blessings at the moment of birth which can at first glance seem so 'unfair'. Why is it that one child is beautiful, clever and born into a wonderful, wealthy family, while another experiences only the most negative sides of life from their early years?

We are all born unequal with unequal opportunities and unequal abilities. It is unfair, but that is just how life is. Philosophers and astrologers both believe that the roots of all this lie in our previous incarnations. Our future depends on how well we cope with the tasks we face in this life.

One of the values of astrology is that it can reveal to us the main purpose of this incarnation. After all, this may be the one that can improve our lives overall. When you analyse a horoscope, you can communicate this information to a person, and often they will say that they sense internally the purpose the astrologer has described. However, communicating the purpose or mission of a person's life is much easier than actually fulfilling it.

Many dismiss the issue altogether preferring to leave the decision 'till later'. And then they come to the end of their life disappointed regretting the opportunities they have missed, certain that they have lived an unhappy life and have somehow failed. The unfinished business of this life will be continued in the next incarnation, and so it goes on until a person has fulfilled that particular life purpose.

For example, the horoscope of one client showed that his main task in life was to have a family. He was an attractive, successful, 37-year-old businessman who worked a lot but was in no hurry to start a family.

"It just hasn't worked out," he said with an embarrassed shrug. "I put so much time and energy into my work, I have nothing left for a personal life."

He was always put off creating a family, was afraid of commitment and did not know what to do about it. Moreover, he was almost never at home. He literally spent all day and night at work. Instinctively, he gave himself to the side of life he took to most easily — his career. Work for him was a convenient shield with which he covered himself, thereby justifying the problems in the personal life. Continuing in this vein, he risked ending his days all alone when he would have no need of the achievements he was so proud of now. And when an astrologer, someone from the outside, speaks of these things, the deepest secrets of our psyche unwittingly rise to the surface revealing all the parts of ourselves that our dodgy consciousness would rather take great pains to hide than to admit. After a conversation like this, people start to think about the true reasons for their behaviour and turn to face the main issues in their life.

A horoscope is incredibly multifaceted. It can tell you everything about a person's character, their health, opportunities, talents and future partners. Whenever a horoscope indicates more than one marriage in a person's life, it always turns out to be the case. And when a partner is shown to be someone of a different nationality or from another country, it always turns out that way.

Interestingly, people of mixed nationalities, for example, a person whose mother is Russian and their father Jewish, often choose partners from abroad. It is as if their already mixed blood calls to be mixed even more. And their children often marry people of a different nationality. The international line is always highlighted in their horoscopes. So it was with my client. Her father was Tatar, her mother Russian, and she married a German.

You can also tell from a horoscope whether a person's marriage will be a happy one or not. In India, where they attach great importance to astrological forecasts, many families order horoscopes for their children and build the child's family life in accordance with the astrologer's indications. I have a friend, who has an excellent knowledge of Indian astrology and customs, and he told me once of a very interesting case.

There was a young man from a wealthy Indian family who was engaged to a girl he was passionately in love with. Everyone complained that the girl was ordinary, while this lad was handsome, smart, rich and upright. The wedding preparations were already underway when suddenly, a month before the happy day, the guy and his parents decided to pull out. It was an unusual incident in Indian society, especially since the family chose not to reveal the reason for their decision.

After some time, the jilted young woman met someone else, who was in some ways similar to her former love, like a brother. He was equally as handsome, charming, smart and rich. And he loved her so much that everyone wondered what it was about this inconspicuous bride that enabled her to attract such amazing young men. This time, the wedding went ahead but the overall happiness only lasted a year. Twelve months after the wedding, the young man died in a car accident. Only then did the parents of the first fiancé explain their reason for breaking off the engagement — they had the future bride's horoscope drawn up and the astrologer had told them that the girl's first husband would die, and that she would be widowed. Naturally, not wanting such a fate to befall their son, they withdrew their consent to the marriage. Evidently, the first fiancé's horoscope showed no such indication. The horoscope of the second groom fully coincided with the tragic scenario but neither he nor his parents had bothered to have his horoscope done, maybe because the young man's fate was such that nothing could have helped him.

You cannot avert a person's death. It is something that can never be changed. The great blind clairvoyant of our time, 'Baba Vanga', and other famous clairvoyants have all said the same thing. Even if a person is repeatedly warned, as was the case with the American President John F. Kennedy, nothing can be done to avert the fate of death. Both astrologers and clairvoyants warned the American President of mortal danger but he went to Texas anyway.

In my own practice, I have only twice warned a client of the possibility of death. In one case, the horoscope spoke of the likelihood of an accident at around the age of 33 years and one month. My client was 32. He ran a large business, was married to his second wife and enjoyed life in every way. He was a pleasant lad, good-looking and clever. And although I was not talking about death but of a traumatic period, he understood the situation very well.

"A gypsy told me about this when I was young," he said after listening attentively. "I guess we'll just have to wait and see." The gypsy had read his palm and I understand why she made the prediction she did. The life line on his right hand was short barely reaching the middle of the palm. The wisdom line was also truncated. And the left hand was an exact copy of the right. I have to say that at the dawn of my predictive practice, I did a lot of palmistry but then it somehow faded into the background. I do sometimes take a look at the lines on a client's hand and they always duplicate the horoscope reading.

Some time later, after he turned 33, the prediction came true. On the 23rd February[2], the young businessman set off to the office expecting his colleagues to celebrate the occasion and suddenly remembered that he had left an important document at home and so he went back. It turned out that he had locked the keys inside the flat and there was no-one else at home. The flat was on the second floor, and so the best he could think of was to climb in through the balcony. He had already

---

[2] Defender of the Fatherland Day, a holiday dedicated to those who served and those who are currently serving in the Armed Forces.

indulged in a few drinks and his coordination was shaky. In the end, he slipped from the balcony and fell to his death.

The second time I was able to predict a dangerous time to the day, and the client was very attentive to the information, especially since they read my books and newspaper forecasts. There was an element of risk involved in his work and, on the day I mentioned, he took all possible precautions. Nevertheless, he was shot and ended up in intensive care, where he spent several days on the verge of life and death. He called me as soon as he regained consciousness, and told me that what I had forecast had come true.

"I died. I was in the other world and then I came back. I saw you there, and you were telling me that it was not my time yet. And then I came back."

It's hard to say why he saw me specifically as I was not thinking about him at the time. I had done my work conscientiously and did not return to his chart afterwards. Six months had passed, and during that time many different clients had come to me with their various problems and concerns. An astrologer does not always remember their clients except their regular clients who come for consultations over a number of years.

This young man was not a regular client. He had only come to see me once and I forgot about him afterwards. Naturally, after this incident, he began to visit me regularly and at one point, he came with his wife. Her horoscope had all the indications of widowhood, and I did not hide the fact. Moreover, there was signs of a controversial property issue and so there was a need to have documents drawn up in his wife's name to avoid unnecessary problems in the future. His wife kept asking me whether it was possible to prevent what was ordained by the heavens.

"After all, it's happened once before," she said hopefully.

We agreed that they would come and see me roughly on a yearly basis, since it is very difficult to draw up a daily horoscope for a long period into the future. It's a challenge to draw up this kind of horoscope for as much as a year but not impossible.

Three years passed happily, and during that time there were many pleasant events in my client's life which I was able to predict. He became wealthy very quickly and he had a son.

Early one year, he did not come and visit as he had before, and then in March his wife called.

"Denis died yesterday. He was killed."

"Why didn't he come and see me in the New Year?"

"Everything was going really well. He was very busy at work and ended up chasing his tail. He kept meaning to call and book an appointment."

Clearly, there was no longer any need for him to visit me. It would not have helped save his life. Or perhaps I would have calculated the fateful day and that would not have helped anyone.

Some psychologists and opponents of astrology believe that negative predictions can come true because the person is expecting a negative outcome. But this is not so. When it comes to an accident, death always comes unexpectedly and quickly, sometimes in a matter of seconds. As the great mystic Mikhail Bulgakov[3] noted, 'Yes, man is mortal, but that would be only half the trouble. The worst of it is that he is sometimes unexpectedly mortal.'

Perhaps death comes to a person when they have completed what they came to do on this earth, or perhaps when they stray too far from their intended path. In this regard, the age of 29 and 33 and the periods 37–42 and 55–56 are highly indicative. For many, this can be a time of dramatic change, when life can begin anew. It is during these periods that people often move to a new home, start a new family or completely change their profession.

These periods in life also coincide with a large proportion of deaths and according to the rules of astrology, this is a time for making choices and evaluating the past. One may of course guess at the mechanisms behind this phenomenon but we cannot know anything for certain. It is even more true that nothing can be done to change it. Chinese wisdom has it that, **"the power of heaven is incomprehensible. It bends and straightens, straightens and bends. It plays with heroes and it breaks giants. And there is no misfortune that does not portend joy"**.

These are truly great words and could replace many hours spent in conversation with a psychologist. Perhaps the next tale will serve to illustrate them.

---

[3] Mikhail Bulgakov was a famous Russian writer best known for his novel "The Master and Margarita"

SHIRIN

Psychologists say that a person's life often plays out similarly to the plot of the fairy-tale they loved most as a child. Perhaps this is the case, for the plot of that fairy tale lives within us and gradually shapes our character and our fate, for fate is indeed nothing more than the unfolding of our own character over time. This is one of the most important postulates of astrology and it perfectly echoes popular wisdom and the sayings, 'a man's character is his fate' or 'sow a character and you reap a destiny.'

If a princess lives inside a woman and remains alive in spite of all life's circumstances, she will certainly end up meeting her long-awaited prince.

The beginning of this woman's life was surprisingly reminiscent of a fairy-tale. She was born into a loving, creative family and by the age of 16 had become a movie star. Fabulously beautiful, tender and charming, she was a true heroine of the Central Asian republic, Uzbekistan, a country in which it is not easy for a woman to hold star-like status. By the age of nineteen, she had featured in several films and received a flattering offer from the Indian movie star Shashi Kapoor who was one of her many devoted admirers. It appeared that good fairies the world over had conspired to pave her way in life with roses without thorns. I saw the films made in those years in which she starred.

She had a light, slender figure, long black plaits and huge almond-shaped eyes with the power to talk and bewitch.

A beautiful life stretched out before her. She had everything: fame, youth, talent and beauty. What more could anyone want? But the gods reasoned differently. 'There are no roses without thorns,' they said, and then they woke up the most evil, cunning fairy of them all who appeared to have forgotten all her other duties. With a single wave of her black wand, the life of this beautiful young woman changed in a heartbeat. It changed as in a fairy tale, when the beautiful maiden is kidnapped by a villain like Koschei the Deathless or Gorynych the Serpent[4].

Our movie star was also kidnapped — kidnapped without care or consent, like girls sometimes are in Central Asian countries. The role of villain was played by the stuntman in a film crew, a 26-year-old lad, half-bandit, half-sportsman. She caught his eye and without thinking too much about it, he 'stole' her and carried her off to his relatives in a mountain village where they carried out the nikah ceremony of a Muslim wedding.

Once a young woman has spent the night with the groom's relatives, there is no going back. Attitudes are that the girl has dishonoured herself and her family and will never marry again. The elderly women, relatives of the groom, guard the bride and instil in her the idea that since she has been 'stolen', this must be her fate and if she leaves the groom's house, Allah will never forgive her and will surely punish her.

---

[4] Archetypal male antagonists in Russian folklore.

The power of tradition is so great, very rarely does a girl who has been 'stolen' return to her home. She is often raped on the first night spent away from her own family and on the rare occasion that a girl does run away, in order to escape the shame, she is forced to leave her home region forever.

This time the situation was complicated by the fact that no one subsequently treated Shirin (that was the name of our beautiful young maiden) any respect. She was taken off to a distant village, to the stuntman's relatives. The stuntman simply raped her that night and, in the morning, the women made her wear a headscarf, which was the symbol of a married woman. Nobody knew where she was or what had happened to her. By the time the truth was finally revealed, Shirin was pregnant. Everyone was afraid of her husband, and no one wanted to have anything to do with him. Shirin accepted her fate and soon gave birth to a son.

That was how the fairy-tale princess was transformed into a genuine Cinderella. She lived in the mountain village together with her husband's relatives and dutifully fulfilled the role expected of an Asian daughter-in-law. And the expectations were many: do all the family's washing, cook for everyone, wash out the dirty, heavy cooking cauldrons, and most importantly, never contradict anyone, learn to be silent, servile and humble.

Young, naive, inexperienced, unused to village life, a complete stranger to such places, in the first years of her marriage Shirin suffered and wept often. Her husband, who soon became bored of his young, beautiful maid set off in search of adventure and seldom returned to the village. Shirin was only too glad that he was often away. She hated him with her whole being, while he beat her, raped her and humiliated her in every possible way.

Five years later, she gave birth to a second son, and a year after that, her husband moved to the capital of Kyrgyzstan, Bishkek, taking Shirin and the children with him. He bought a huge house at the foot of the mountains, did it up and carried on with his life. Shirin had no idea how he spent his time. She could only guess that he had some illegal, half-gangster business. A great lover of antiquity, he brought home expensive antiques and their mansion began to resemble a museum.

Life became somewhat easier. There was more money around, their sons were getting older and there were none of her husband's hateful relatives around to torment her. From time to time, her husband had other women, a fact which he did not try to conceal from her. Insolent, rude and lecherous, he brought them into the home, where he held orgies in true bacchanalian style. This went on while the children were still little but once they reached a certain age, the orgies ceased. In his own way, the husband loved his children and did not want them to witness his atrocities. Shirin was a stranger to him and he treated her and the entire female sex in bestial manner. It was impossible for her to leave him. He had warned her once and for all that if she even thought about running away, he would never see her again, and good riddance, but the boys would stay with him. Shirin could not leave the children. They were her life. The boys were handsome, talented, and loved their mother very much. It was their love that saved Shirin from depression, sorrow and worst of all, the loss of any will to live.

Another long, ten years passed. Over this time, Shirin changed hugely. She lost the radiant, sparkling beauty that her fans had once so admired. Nevertheless, she managed not to let herself go and remained just as light, aristocratic, refined and contained in manner. She never complained to anyone, and no-one knew her story. At the age of 30, she started working as a television journalist. By this time, she and her husband lived like strangers under the same roof. He had his own room, while she and the boys had theirs. They had a live-in nanny, an elderly Russian woman, who helped Shirin with the housework. The nanny loved Shirin dearly and felt much sympathy for her.

I met Shirin when she was 35 years old. She called, introduced herself and asked to come and see me. At that time, astrology in our country was just beginning to emerge from the world of underground culture, and Shirin wanted to make a program about astrologers and the astrology centre we had founded in Bishkek. It was an interesting project and I agreed without hesitation. Naturally, I did not know anything about her then or her past but I instantly noticed her pleasant appearance, fine taste, gentle aristocratic manners and a certain innate artistry that imparted a distinguished quality to all her movements. She looked worn out, exhausted and not entirely in good health. She totally lacked the bold presumptuous manner characteristic of many journalists. But Shirin was good at her job, and the program turned out well.

After that, she became a frequent guest to our office and once very delicately asked if I would draw up her horoscope. I was surprised to learn that she was only 35. Her exhausted look gave the impression of someone much older. It was as if the life force was slowly leaving her slender, graceful body, giving way to some mysterious concealed ailment.

Born under the sign of Libra, Shirin took good care of herself, practiced yoga and often went on various kinds of diet. Her problems did not lie in the physical body though. It was the emotional stress she had first experienced 15 years earlier and years of suffering and humiliation that had taken their toll. In her case, it was not the body that cried out for healing but the soul.

Her forecast was optimistic - in two years time, at the age of 37, there was a chance that her life would change. Her chart showed indications of a trip abroad, love, divorce and a new, completely different life.

"Pure fantasy," Shirin whispered incredulously. "How could that be possible? But thank you anyway."

She told me the story of her past and brought in several films for me to watch in which she had once shone as an actress. I could not believe my eyes. Could that young, beautiful woman who was full of life really be the same person as this worn out, timid woman?

Once, Shirin invited us to her home. Her husband was away and we were met by the hostess herself and a short, elderly Russian woman. Two handsome, dark-haired boys stared at their mother's guests in curiosity. The house itself left a strange, disturbing impression. The dark red carpet on the stairs was the colour of hardened blood stains. The house was filled with dark, antique, inconceivably expensive furniture and Persian carpets, and the gloomy walls were hung with old embroideries in dark cherry colours. It all created an atmosphere of anxiety and despondence. There were ancient jugs in the courtyard, that looked like they originated in the stone Age, and large eastern-style cauldrons and behind it all the moody mountains towered directly above the fence. How anyone could live in such a house was a mystery to me. It was as if those walls had seen everything it was possible to see bar joy and happiness.

We had dinner in the courtyard beneath an old, wide-branched apricot tree. Even when it was getting dark and there was a chill in the evening air, we did not want to go back inside.

The boys stared at us intrigued by the "living" astrologer-visitor and listened to every word. The oldest was 14 and he had the look of an oriental prince from an ancient-ancient fairy tale... Attentive, thoughtful, very handsome, he was interested in religion, philosophy, and was studying martial arts and music. His interests were radically different from those of his father. He loved and understood animals, and he kept snakes. They did not bite him, and he was not at all afraid of them. There were snakes in the nearby mountains and he had caught his own snakes there and taken them home with him.

The youngest was 9 years old and strongly resembled his mother. It was obvious that the children adored Shirin, and she changed dramatically in their presence appearing instantly younger, prettier, laughing cheerfully.

The huge, dark, roomy house was foreign to them, although they had lived there for many years. Their tyrannical father's grim creation now seemed empty and abandoned. And it was strange but I had a strong feeling that these three would not be living there for much longer. The possibility of a different future was already in the air, enveloping their faces and figures. There was no longer any connection between the people and the house. It was as if the wind might blow at any moment and carry them all away to another happier place, to another happier future.

The evening came to an end and after that Shirin became a more frequent guest at the office. With her help, we made several programs about astrology, which aroused interest among the general public. It is not to say that we were close friends, but there was a pleasant kind of connection between us that people sometimes have when they find each other's company interesting and do not necessarily want anything more from each other.

Later, I moved to Moscow and we lost contact. A year and a half after that, Shirin called me from Switzerland. She had accompanied a group of businessmen and a television crew abroad in her capacity as a journalist, and quite out of the blue had met a smart, cultured, high-ranking Swiss gentleman. Her oriental appearance, almond-shaped eyes and exquisite manners had a profound effect on him, and the gentleman suggested that the beautiful journalist stay with him in Switzerland. When love is real, it knows no obstacles and quite to her own surprise and to the surprise of her entire team, Shirin stayed behind in Switzerland.

The man was 14 years older than her and came from an aristocratic family of many generations — his grandfather used to be the country's president. It was not possible for them to marry straight away as Shirin was already married, and she faced a difficult divorce process. The boys lived in Central Asia and arranging their relocation would be a huge challenge.

However, what needs to happen always happens in the end. Hidden forces must have been helping Shirin because she achieved the impossible. She managed to separate without her husband's knowledge and secretly secure her sons' relocation to her new home in Switzerland.

Returning one day after another escapade, the head of the family and father of two sons found the house empty, abandoned by all. It took him a long time to work out where his wife and children were and by the time he did, it was too late. Many, many years later, he finally got what he deserved and retribution came in the same form as his original crime. The Indians say, 'what goes away always comes back.' According to the law of karma, everyone gets exactly what they deserve, no more, no less. And these words too are always true, 'Don't delude yourself. God won't be mocked. As you sow, so shall you reap.'

Shirin called me from time to time. All was well with her. Her husband was loving and was good to the children. Always having lacked fatherly attention, the boys quickly got used to him. They attended the best school in Switzerland where they were no doubt happy.

I recently travelled to Switzerland and met up with Shirin whilst I was there. We met on the Montreux Promenade in an oriental restaurant at her husband's invitation. He was a calm, pleasant man, who at first glance looked no more than 45. He knew about the forecast I had made more than seven years earlier and was surprised at how accurate it was.

"How could you have known? It all happened so unexpectedly for Shirin and myself."

Shirin had changed hugely. A stable life with a man who loved her had done its work. She was calmer and more self-confident. Aristocratic and refined, she was returned to her former life, the fairy-tale life of a princess. In spite of everything that she had been forced to endure, in her heart she had remained a princess, and so had ended up returning to the kind of environment that was most natural to her. The gods had tested her endurance and she had proven herself worthy.

Do my clients' stories always have a happy ending? Unfortunately not. Some you might say are like 'dead-end' stories. It seems impossible to make rational sense or find the meaning in them... Perhaps there is a meaning to these stories but one which can only be seen from 'somewhere above,' where other laws and a different heavenly logic reign.

A Woman's Life and Love

There are days when the air itself seems heavy, oppressive and downright depressing. It is often on days like this that the clients who come to see bring complex, stuck situations, which seem to have no reasonable explanation.

It was on just such a day as this that my next female client appeared. She had a pleasant appearance, was tastefully dressed and at first glance appeared totally calm. There was no fuss or anxiety to her, just an even, quiet voice and measured movements. However, it was not the same calm that strong, confident people have. On the contrary, the woman's whole appearance was as if covered in the dull ashes of hopelessness and total acceptance of her fate. Her large grey eyes were filled with such longing that there was something eerie about her. In a flat voice lacking intonation, she gave me the details of her birth and clearly did not intend to give any explanation as to why she had come. Evidently, I was not the first to whom she had turned for help, and it looked as if her previous visits to clairvoyants and fortunetellers had all been unsuccessful. In a case like this, the best approach is to silently carry out your work and then express your own thoughts about the supposed purpose of the visit. This is the only way to gain a client's trust and encourage a more frank conversation.

This woman's horoscope spoke of serious problems in her marriage, which would last for at least another two and a half years. So what happened? Most likely an extra-marital affair after which the marriage had somehow been preserved. At the same time, the difficult situation was ongoing; it was likely that the husband was still dividing his attention between the two women. When I talked about all this, the client nodded silently without commenting on my assumptions.

Her husband's horoscope spoke of a serious infatuation that had begun about three years previously. His chart indicated a relationship with a woman involving a significant age difference, a woman who was much older than his wife. They would not get divorced. Of that I was certain. The question was how and when the whole affair would end that was clearly so torturous for all involved. The chart showed a positive move both for my client and her husband a year and a half to two years in the future. This was potentially a positive solution for her and so I began our conversation with this information.

It was clear that the situation had long been out in the open, and my client responded very calmly to the story of her husband's mistress. Her response was normal for someone finding themselves in a situation that had already been experienced and negotiated many times.

"Yes, I know her well," my client smirked. "The other woman is my mother."

I had to make an effort not to show my surprise. Her mother?! It turned out that my client had suffered the betrayal not only of her husband but of the person she was closest to in the world, her own mother! Like a bird shot at from both sides, there was nowhere for her to fly. Now I understood the melancholy in her eyes and aura of complete despair.

"So, now that you know all the details, can you tell me how this will all end?"

"You and your husband will move away and that will put an end to it all. You won't get divorced."

"A divorce is out of the question. We have three children and I don't work. I got married very young and have no training. I am just a wife and a mother. He has a good salary and so we are comfortably off and anyway, he will never be separated from the children. As for me, I'm just an extension of the kids, a convenient extension. And while they are little, there is nothing I can do to change the situation. So you think we'll move. How soon?"

"In about a year and a half to two years, you'll move abroad. I don't know which country exactly. For now, it looks as if this unnatural connection will continue."

"Is there nothing I can do?"

"I fear not."

"You have no idea how much money I've spent on clairvoyants who've promised me he'll leave her. But they are still seeing each other and there's nothing anyone can do about it."

Gradually, my client began to open up and I learned the details of her strange story. She married passionately in love at the age of 19. Two years later she had a son and two years afterwards a daughter. There was an interval of another two years before her youngest daughter was born. Everything was fine between them initially. Her husband worked hard and she brought up the children. The children took up all her time and energy and became the most important part of her life. After the birth of the third daughter, my client's mother became a more frequent guest to their home. She helped with the children and was the ideal grandmother.

"She has aged well and is still very beautiful," the daughter sighed.

When they had family get-togethers, the mother often danced with her son-in-law, and as everyone noted, they looked great together.

"My father and I used to watch them and joke: 'they are both so lively, young and interesting, and we are both so wise, calm and serious."

And no-one noticed anything more until one day, the father returned home much earlier than usual. He calmly unlocked the door to his own apartment only to be met by strange sounds which could only mean one thing. In the conjugal bed, his wife was making love to their son-in-law. The passion between the two was so strong, they did not immediately notice my client's father. But he slowly sank to the floor and fell so ill that his wife had to call an ambulance.

Without saying a word to anyone else, my client's father left his wife. It was a long time before his daughter learned the reason for her parents' divorce. He felt sorry for his daughter and assumed that the lovers would come to their senses and that things would settle down. But that did not happen and the daughter found out for herself when she caught her mother and her husband kissing. Both her relationship with her mother and married life as she had known it totally broke down. Her husband did not try and deny anything. In fact, he was very blunt.

"Yes, we love each other and have no intention of separating. Unlike you, your mother is a real woman. I only ever slept with you because you are so like your mother."

Things went on like this for another eighteen months and during this time my client went through all the rounds of hell. When her husband did not come home at night, she knew exactly where he was and with whom. He jokingly explained to his wife that she should accept the situation because 'even in Ancient Rome, emperors cohabited with all their relatives'. Life became unbearable and there were times when she seriously considered ending it all. The only thing that kept her going was the fact that the children were little and still needed her constant care and attention. She tried to leave with the children once but her husband stopped her.

"You can go wherever you like but I won't let you take the children. They need a father, and you won't be able to bring them up or feed them without my help."

All my client's efforts to find work were in vain. Her husband was a well known figure in the city and no-one would have given her employment without his consent. They were considered to be the perfect couple and no-one suspected anything. The children adored their father and gradually, my client came to accept things as they were. She resigned herself to circumstances but profound feelings of despair took root in her soul. She could not talk to anyone about it, after all, her rival was her own mother! My client had a recurring dream in which she was drowning in a dark, raging river and desperately trying to grab hold of the riverbank and then the terror would wake her up.

That was when she started making countless visits to grandmother-fortunetellers, many of whom promised to return her husband to her but nothing did the trick. He kept on seeing her mother. Once, exhausted after another sleepless night, she went to see a gypsy-woman, an imperious old woman. Rumour had it that she was a black witch and could do anything.

"I am actually a person of faith but I just so wanted to put a stop to it once and for all. She took almost all my jewellery from me but did nothing."

It has to be said that women who lose their husbands or lovers to another tend to be very trusting and can fall like flies into the web of all kinds of sorcerers and charlatans. They will give anything to get their beloved back and this naivety is artfully exploited by those individuals who sometimes call themselves magicians or representatives of God on earth.

All those magic salons hung with icons! Who knows what goes on in the name of the holy ones! I spoke once with a clairvoyant woman, who received her clients in a fashionable salon of magic.

"Yes, I can change a person's fate," she told me confidently.

"No one but the Almighty can change a person's fate."

"He has given me the powers. I can influence the course of a person's life."

What can you say to that? Such confidence comes from unbridled ignorance and monstrous conceit. And this woman promises to return a lost love, to draw wealth and fame into a person's life and create all sorts of other miracles. If only it was all that simple! We could all just hand over a heap of cash and live happily ever after! The future can be foretold but it cannot be changed, not in that manner at least. The only way the future can be changed is by changing oneself and that is the hardest work on Earth.

My client continued her story.

"Nobody could help me and now you are saying that it's all going to carry on as before. This is no life. Only now do I understand what it means to be a 'living corpse'. I ought to hate him but I don't. I still love him and I still hope that one day I'll wake up and this nightmare will be over. He is the only man I have ever known and I can't imagine my life without him. My mother is dead to me now. I don't even think about her any more. It's as if she no longer exists."

What advice can one possibly give to a person in a situation like this? 'Look after yourself? Do something for yourself, anything'? She had already done that, learned languages attended courses in design. All she needed from me now was an astrological forecast, nothing more. A move was the only way out of the situation, perhaps not the most joyful but, nonetheless, it was something.

After she had gone, I was left with the feeling that something had been taken from me. I felt exhausted and could not understand why this woman, a good, honest person, a faithful wife and beautiful mother was having to go through all this. As an astrologer, I understood the reason for what was happening perfectly but the human being in me raised her head and started arguing with the astrologer.

"What is the point in all this? So that she can forget herself, cease to be her own person, lose herself totally in her children? Is that what all this is about? Is that not a woman's most important purpose?" This was the voice of the woman and human being in me.

"But you know very well," the astrologer objected, "that intimate relationships can be cruel on an energetic level. It is always important to keep a balance in a relationship and maintain a sense of one's own self, otherwise, there is no-one there left to love. There is only one truth in this scenario — the person who gets abandoned is always the one to blame, as they end up having nothing left to offer their partner. This woman has to suffer in order to change and remember that she too has needs."

"Yes, but whatever part of the blame lies with her, the punishment is truly awful," the human being in me said empathising with the woman.

An astrologer might often feel empathy for a client but this should never interfere with the work at hand. For this reason, I make a point of not working with those closest to me, especially my children. When one works with people who are very close, one's perception is blurred and the forecast can end up being either excessively optimistic or un-justifiably pessimistic. In these cases, it is better to recommend a col-league whom you know and trust.

Why was this man so attracted to the mother? Why this strange, unnatural choice? Astrologers know that a man is often attracted to women of the same type, and sometimes a man's first and second wife will be similar, as if they were sisters. Sometimes, they will even share the same name. This story was another example of the same tendency — the mother was a more interesting, more colourful version of the daughter. The horoscopes of both women were very similar. Both were born under the sign of Cancer but the mother was more independent, more dynamic and charming and she had something that always fascinates men, that quality they call 'eternal femininity'. Age did not come into it. People will always be attracted to whoever is energetically the more powerful. The daughter had stopped identifying with herself as a woman. She had given herself exclusively to the role of mother and had no interest in anything beyond her children. It is no coincidence that the affair began after the birth of the third child.

In the life of the husband, one energy had been replaced by another that was similar but stronger. It was not that his image of the ideal woman had changed, it was that his wife was no longer a match for him. The husband was an Aquarius and this sign occurred in the eighth house of both his wife's and her mother's charts. The eighth house rules death, destruction, transformation, and usually this type of union brings with it a sea of passion and suffering. So it was in this case. The husband had destroyed his own family and the family of his lover, his mother-in-law. In addition, for many Aquarius men when it comes to sexual relationships anything goes. To some extent they are 'rogues'.

When a man meets another woman who is the same star sign as his existing wife, it almost always leads to divorce because one energy is squeezed out by another energy that is similar. This often happens in life because a person tends to be attracted to the same type of energy in others. Sometimes, in addition to the zodiac sign, both the old and the new partner will share the same name — names also carry a particular vibration.

Once, in a live TV program, one of the viewers asked the following question:

"My first wife was called Tatyana and she was a Capricorn. I'm now seeing a woman who is also called Tatyana and she is also a Capricorn. Will I end up marrying her?"

It was not possible to draw up the man's chart right there and then but an appropriate answer lay in the question itself:

"Yes, you will marry her." Some time passed and that same gentleman tracked me down. He had indeed married the woman he had been seeing and they were both happy. The man recounted how his relationship in the second marriage had initially begun to develop in the same way as his earlier relationship but he managed to change his own behaviour and consequently build a second, more harmonious family.

"It's like I'm re-sitting a year going over the same curriculum correcting my old mistakes," he said.

How well he understood the situation!

Many women are guilty of the same mistake. They push their husbands away by prioritising the children, domestic issues and their girlfriends. They forget that a man is just like the children and needs attention, just as they do. Selfish, maternal heroism along the lines of 'everything for children' and 'nothing for myself' to say nothing of one's partner does not actually help anyone, not least the children. All children really need is for their parents to be happy.

A situation in which the mother is always exhausted on account of the sacrifices she makes and barely notices the father is always fraught with infidelity and family conflict. The 'you be the nanny and I'll be the breadwinner' scheme does not suit all husbands. Aside from that, they want to feel that they are still a man and lover to their wife. And if the woman does not require these qualities of her husband, he will always find somewhere else where they are.

Sometimes, a woman will play a different game in which she tries her best to be the ideal mother. She is driven by the desire to assert herself and prove that she can do what is needed better than anyone else. She enjoys playing the key role and step by step methodically distances the father from the children's upbringing. Gradually, he becomes a stranger in the family and realises that all they need from him is money. Many men stay in a family in which they feel unloved and restless. But people (at least the majority of us) cannot live without love and will end up finding it somewhere else. Love is a powerful means of energy exchange. It is the only thing that keeps people together and while there is love in a relationship, the couple will stay together. In this case, affairs are very rare and are unlikely to be an issue at all.

The above is not meant to justify adultery so much as to explain why it happens in the first place. Of course, it is easy to say, 'what a bastard' but what is the good in that? All this I expressed to my client who came to the office a week later. She was already aware of her problem and had thought about it a lot. The tragedy taking place in her family had caused her to rethink many areas of her life.

"I lived like a blade of grass or a plant and never had interests or a life of my own. Nobody took my needs into consideration. Pain has forced me to change. I am still changing and I have no idea where it will take me." It was a good thing that my client understood her tragedy in this way and was interpreting the pain as a signal for change and transformation. She would be all right now that she had succeeded in getting to the root of things, as with that she had found a way forward.

I did not see her for a long time but a year and a half later, she came to see me again.

She and her husband had moved. He had found reliable partners abroad who were offering him a part in their business. He could not turn down such an advantageous offer, especially since the economic situation in the country was looking far from rosy and his own business was rapidly losing momentum.

For the business-minded, pragmatic type of person that he was, business was more important than everything else, and he agreed to the move. His mother-in-law-lover stayed did not move with them. The laws of the country to which they had moved did not allow it. So the son-in-law and the mother separated never to see each other again.

A year later, my client returned to organise the sale of what remained of their property and she came to see me. She was still living with her husband and their relationship had improved slightly. Sometimes he slept in her bedroom but she always had the impression that in his thoughts, he was still with her mother. And perhaps he was. She forgave him, though, and let go of her anger towards him.

The pain might have gone but still, she had made the decision to leave him when the children were grown up. Her horoscope indicated that she would meet someone else six or seven years later and marry for a second time. By then, she would be 46 and her second marriage would be a happy one. She did not visit her mother whilst she was in the country but she learned from her father that her mother lived alone and hardly ever saw anyone.

What did her mother feel? Was her loneliness retribution for betraying her own daughter or was it just that she no longer needed anyone? Was her passion so strong that she could abandon her daughter, her grandchildren and her husband with whom she had shared so many years without regret? We will never know the answer to this question but of all the people involved in this story, only she ended up totally alone. One might suppose that the isolation and loneliness which she experienced later in life was payment for the mistakes she had made. Her husband remarried well and her daughter stayed with her husband and subsequently would be happy with another. Her lover son-in-law was already looking at other women with undisguised interest. The grandchildren would grow up and their mother would make sure that they never had any communication with their grandmother.

Did she regret what happened or did she think that five years of love was a worthy reward for her subsequent loneliness? Whatever the case, this story is difficult to understand and has the tone of a divine but ugly joke that broke the lives of four different people. In the East, love is thought of as a disease or a disaster that befalls a person. However, few can walk away from love and why should they?

Over the years of my practice, I have only once heard a story of a person walking away from love, motivated, as it might at first appear by a strong sense of duty and responsibility for another.

Once a woman came to see me, who I had been recommended to by friends. She was 49 years old, and looked tired, grey and somehow 'unplugged'. She wanted to know about the future of her relationship with her husband. However, the stubborn chart stated unequivocally that the relationship no longer existed and had broken down a long time ago, 10 to 11 years ago to be precise. The event that signalled the beginning of the end of their harmonious life together had taken place in the distant past. It was a case of love, true love and I asked my client about it directly.

"Yes, eleven years ago, I met the man who was probably my other half. We worked together and understood each other perfectly. It took me a while to work out that I was in love. Although, no, I think I knew but was in denial. I kept telling myself that we were just friends. It was easier that way. My husband is a good man and I have a wonderful daughter. We have a good life and a circle of mutual friends. There came a time though when I had to make a choice. It took me a while to get there because I could not imagine my life without that other person. I chose my husband, and at that time it seemed the natural, rational thing to do. Why destroy the family? Why change anything? My husband and daughter had done nothing wrong. I made the decision I did for their sake but missed the other man terribly and thought about him every moment of every day. Whatever I did, he was invisibly present in my soul.

They say time heals, but time went by and nothing changed. I longed for him and thought constantly about the fact that we had never been intimate together. We had never even kissed. Gradually, it became a disease, an obsession. I was irritable, quick-tempered, and everything my husband did annoyed me although he was attentive, caring, and gentle. He knew what had happened and valued my actions highly. There were no secrets between us and we trusted each other, but it would have been unfair to talk to him about my love and constant longing for another man. And when he was sleeping, I would look at him and think about how I could be lying in bed with another...

Five years passed, and my husband experienced something similar. He chose not to be with a woman he had unexpectedly begun to have feelings for. She lived in a different city, and there was a time when he might have left to go and live with her but he chose not to. He remembered the sacrifice I had made on his behalf.

We are still living together but there is no affection between us now. He is closed off in his own thoughts and feelings as I am in mine. Time has passed and now all trace of mutual gratitude has gone. We are strangers to each other and every evening we look at each other with empty eyes and exchange empty phrases ... Then we go to our own rooms and so it goes on day after day after day. We have not slept together for a long time. We have no desire to touch each other. What does the future hold for me and for him? And why has this happened to us?"

'God alone knows why this has happened to you,' I thought. He had set this woman a difficult task — to learn to love, to live naturally and freely, not to suppress one's desires for the sake of doing what is considered right and respectable but to live by the call of the heart. The woman was far too analytical and had planned her life the way a grandmaster plans a chess game. Now that her well-conceived plans had come to nothing, perhaps she would start to see things in a different light.

Unfortunately, the forecast showed that for now nothing would change. They would not separate but there would be no increase in the warmth between them either. They would separate in two or three years and her husband would initiate the split.

"Will there ever be love in my life again?" she asked hopefully.

"Not like before, no, but there will be a different kind of love. A year from now someone new will enter your life and meeting this person could be life-changing but I can't say for certain how you will respond to the opportunity and whether you'll feel able to face the inevitable difficulties it will bring and finally go with what your heart is telling you."

She shrugged and with a note of irony said, "Why is it that my act of morality and my husband's heroic behaviour have led to such an unfortunate end? Where is the logic and justice in that? Why is it that despite having kept God's commandments, we are both now so unhappy?"

Many people deceive themselves when it comes to their motivations for a certain action. Sometimes people lack the courage to do what they are meant to do but cannot admit it even to themselves. The imagination can be very helpful in finding ways of justifying one's own cowardice.

I remember one particularly prudent man who suddenly found love bursting into his life. He did not know what to do about it and was terrified that his quiet life had come to an end. He was far too happy with the woman he had fallen in love with and very unhappy with his own wife. He was afraid of the love that would inevitably change his life, and 'prudently' decided that this woman could not possibly be quite as wonderful as she seemed. He allowed others to slander her as it was easier for him to turn his back on love and return to his old life. But you can't deceive yourself endlessly. Having rejected love, he lost all interest in life and became hardened and indifferent. His old world ended up falling apart and life itself forced him to acknowledge his mistake.

When we are on the right track in life, we are happy and healthy. This is the only vector that enables a person to stay on track but it can be exceptionally difficult to follow. There is a reason people say that one has to fight for one's happiness in life. But when we do, the reward is great.

When a person deliberately hangs on to a situation often something unusual happens to make them let go of it. The situation blows up of its own accord and gives a person a nudge in the direction they are meant to be going in.

I forecast a move once for a lady who was herself thinking along these lines. The opportunity to make a move had arisen already. Her relatives had long been offering their help and suggesting she come and live with them. Her horoscope eloquently spoke of change, a move, a new life and new friends but the woman was stubborn and dragged things out reluctant to change her life. Then one day, there was a torrential flood in the town where she lived that took my client's home and the shop she owned. And so she moved, but under very different and more complicated circumstances.

But let us return to our very moral heroine. After all, in this case, too, love was sacrificed not for the sake of the woman's husband and daughter but for the sake of an existing life-style that was settled and comfortable.

Born under the sign of Capricorn with a strong Saturn in the ascendant indicated too much stability and inertia of thinking, when the criteria for action is always 'a bird in the hand is worth two in the bush'. And what was it she said, 'why change anything?'!

People like this only dream of change but in reality, they will always hold onto the old. Being this way causes them suffering but they cannot seem to help themselves. They are spectators, who enjoy watching how others love, suffer, separate, quit their old job and start all over again. Sometimes I get the impression that there are two kinds of people in life, players and spectators. The former really live life unafraid to take the blows and answer to their actions, and, as a rule, they achieve their goals. The latter watch the former with surprise and envy, and when they see them winning, they applaud enthusiastically, and when they see someone lose, they will happily curse them with bell, book and candle.

There will always be a reason not to change anything, and the reason will always be a noble one. Many simply cannot imagine themselves truly happy, and at the very last moment, when the prize is in reach, they start looking for reasons to justify their cowardice. But life hates stability. There is either forward or backward movement, nothing in between. To have something and keep it in a totally unchanging condition — really? Crises always happen to people who put all their effort into resisting change. It can be a very painful process, when one's old, established reality literally crumbles into bits. There can be no happy families without love just as there can be no happy people without love. Love can change and take on different forms: for example, unbridled passion might with time transform into a steadily burning flame but it will still be love of the kind when you realise that you simply cannot live without that person. And if this woman had chosen love, she would never have ended up in such a sorrowful situation. But there is no point in thinking about the 'what ifs'. She had already made her decision and was now genuinely confused as to why she had been dealt this hand in life. She spoke of logic, justice and the ten commandments.

There was love in this woman's soul and she had strangled it with her own hands and now genuinely believed that the kind old Lord should be rewarding her for her 'good deed'. As I see it, though, adultery is more like when two people spend a life together without love but are joined by an arrangement of mutual interests. Love, when it is the real thing, can never be a sin.

The expert on human souls, Dr. Freud said, "To live, a person must be able to love and to work."

Why does love play such an important role in our lives? Is it possible to live without it? Probably, but one would never feel fulfilled and truly alive.

The saying, 'When love disappears from a marriage, love appears outside the marriage,' reflects a sound observation. If all had been well in my client's life, this would never have happened in the first place. But how was I to explain all this to her, when she was so convinced of her own infallibility? How was I to nudge her towards the needs of her soul without injuring or offending her? She clearly had a mathematical mind, and so I turned to logic for help.

I began cautiously.

"According to your chart, you are a steady, stable person for whom any change in life is difficult."

"Yes, that's true."

"And when the man you were in love with suggested that you leave your husband and move in with him, did it scare you?"

"Yes."

"So, answering honestly, might one say that you were thinking not so much of your husband and daughter but of yourself? About how constant your own feelings were, how stable his love may or may not be, how you would survive and what your friends and acquaintances would say?"

"Well, on the whole, yes, but I was thinking of my husband and daughter, too."

"Your daughter was already eighteen years old, practically her own person, and would probably have understood. Does she still live with you by the way?"

"No, she got married a long time ago and has her own home now."

"And your husband would eventually have found another."

"Yes, probably."

"Forgive me, but I wonder whether the reason you did not choose love was because it would have meant shaking the foundations of your entire life, which was something you were not ready to do. And not just at that time. This is your attitude towards life as a whole. I get the impression that you are led by the subconscious desire to leave everything as it is. It is always scary, terrifying in fact for you to take any step in the direction of a new life."

"Yes, that's true, but it's natural isn't it?"

"It is natural for you, and you got what you wanted, which was stability. You asked God for stability and he gave it to you. If you had wanted love, he would have given you love. After all, you had the choice. You weighed everything up and in the end got exactly what you wanted. We always receive the thing that we are focused on inwardly. And you find yourself in this condition now because you are not yet ready for another. But in a year from now, you will be at the beginning of a new life cycle which will bring you many new opportunities should you be able to make the most of them. It will be a completely different time and life will be generous towards you."

"A year from now? Won't it be too late, after all, I'm already fifty. But in a sense you are right. I could never even change my job, although there were many opportunities to do so. Sometimes I look back on my life and think of it as an entire series of missed opportunities."

"Do you want to carry on living as you are now?"

"No, and I will think about it, especially as I don't particularly like your forecast about my husband. I don't want to be alone."

We talked some more about her future, her daughter, her husband and all the things people want to discuss when they come to see an astrologer. She left, leaving behind her a feeling of vague dissatisfaction. And again, there was some discontentment with the consultation and the conclusions that had to be drawn.

And so why did the actions of these two individuals lead to the circumstances they faced? Will the dilemma that Anna Karenina and Tatyana Larina faced always remain unsolvable? Both lost, after all. One because she had everything, the other because she turned everything down.

It is hard not to be envious of those who meet their true love when they are young and like in a fairy-tale, spend the rest of their lives together, and die on the same day. Are there many couples like that you might wonder. Every year, there are fewer and fewer. Maybe because time is flowing in a completely different way now, much faster, and people are changing faster. When you bump into someone you have not seen for years, you can see that they are completely different. You look back and understand that you too are not at all the person you used to be. These days, it is as if people live several lives in one lifetime. And each interval requires a different partner. Especially if one person is constantly improving and evolving, while the other is treading water and just marking time. Or maybe our ancestors simply knew how to combine the hidden sides of life with more official scenarios. As the saying goes, 'the family has its place, and love, if it arises, has its place'. And they also went to church, believed in God and read the ten commandments and subtly remarked, 'if you never sin, you'll never repent'.

It seems to me that people have become bolder and more sincere. They express their feelings more openly and, for the most part, do not want to live a lie. Imagine living for years with your husband and all the time dreaming of another! Even if you can manage to hide it, the family's energy field is already compromised. Spiritual betrayal is much worse than physical betrayal, which can be random and not especially significant. But unfulfilled desires can destroy any relationship for they contain both unspent power and the phenomenal attraction of the eternal dream. When a person begins to mentally scroll through a love relationship with another partner, it takes a lot more energy than if it were really happening. Thoughts are material, and an unrealised desire, especially one associated with the call of sex, is always destructive. Naturally, we are talking about real love, not casual relationships that only last for a day. When one person is lost in fantasy, they can make their partner feel cold and uncomfortable as if they were living with a plastic dummy or a living corpse. And so, my client's husband, did what any normal person would do and fell in love with another.

However, not everything in life is always so sad. There are much happier stories of happy couples, too, whose life turned out very differently. Here begins the next story, which in my opinion, represents a worthy contrast to the previous two.

SERGEY

A friend of mine, a strong-willed and talented individual, once asked me to help him understand a complex situation that had developed at work. I conscientiously drew up a chart and answered his questions. That aside, the horoscope unequivocally indicated great changes of a personal nature — a new love, passion and marriage. It was this topic and not the work situation which would become his main concern in the very near future.

Normally, I only answer the questions that interest the client but in this case, I decided to make an exception as, firstly, the changes were going to be truly huge, and, secondly, I knew this person well. Having heard out my suppositions, Sergey (as we shall call him here) smiled incredulously and shrugged as if to say, 'time will tell'.

He did not have to wait long. Barely three months had passed before the events I had predicted started to manifest. Sergey managed a large construction company and was commissioned to make major repairs to the central hospital. There was a huge amount of work to be done and the head physician, an older lady, wise by experience, allocated my friend a separate office so that he could get on with managing the construction site in peace.

His office windows looked directly onto the windows of the neighbouring hospital building, and every day Sergey saw a young, strict-looking female cardiologist making her early morning rounds. She was undoubtedly very beautiful, thin, pale-skinned with slanting, dark brown eyes and had a dazzling, completely 'un-medical' smile. Waves of black hair pushed out prettily from underneath her white cap, and patients took her appearance on the ward as a positive sign for a speedy recovery.

It was love at first sight, or at least, after three days, Sergei had inquired after the beautiful stranger. The information he received was disappointing. She was married and what is more, she was 'seriously married'. She had two little boys and her husband held a senior position in the military. Her name was Indira and she came from an eastern, multinational family belonging to the intelligentsia, in which Kazakh, Tatar and Uzbek blood were intricately intertwined.

The situation seemed hopeless. There never seemed to be an opportunity to even say hello and introduce himself. Indira spent all day with her patients and then a car arrived to pick her up from work and she left.

Not being the kind of person to give up at the first hurdle, Sergei began to plan a happy coincidence. The problem with coincidences is that they are practically impossible to plan. Vaguely aware of this, all Sergey could think of was to pretend he was unwell. Once, while chatting with the head doctor, Sergey grabbed at his heart and effectively pretended to be having a heart attack. He was a good actor and alarmed the head physician who instantly called the cardiologist. The young woman carried out the necessary procedures, listened to his heart and raising her black eyebrows in surprise said that it was nothing serious. He plaintively asked her to sit with him and measure his pulse again.

His heart was actually beating fiercely and his pulse was uneven so closely did those white hands move around him, so closely did those beautiful eyes look at him! Indira prescribed some sedatives, politely said goodbye and left. That was how they met. However, when Sergey repeated the act a second time, a different doctor came to the rescue, who stated dryly that there was absolutely nothing wrong with his heart.

He had come to a dead-end and Sergey did not know what to do next. Raised according to oriental tradition, Indira was always polite but at the same time, cold and inaccessible. She did not get his hints and did not react at all to admiring glances and compliments. Time passed, but no matter how hard Sergey tried, he could not move things on.

However, he was one of those rare people who can achieve practically anything they set their minds to. At school, he was a small, inconspicuous kid but he set himself the goal of growing taller and with heroic effort achieved his goal. He hung for hours from a horizontal bar, which he built himself. He went to basketball training and, despite his short stature, became one of the best players on the team. In the ninth grade, he was 156 centimetres tall. Three years later, he was already 175. His family struggled and he worked hard to help his father but at the same time he studied well and without any outside support got a place at college. He had a great voice, played the guitar, had an amazing sense of humour and could be the life and soul of any group. Besides all this, he was good-looking and had a certain male attractiveness that always won women over. Fair-haired and blue-eyed, he could have had any woman he wanted but to his misfortune, he fell in love with another man's wife.

Six months passed, and during this time Sergey found out everything there was to know about Indira, how she lived, what she liked, who her friends were and where she spent her time. As a young woman, almost a girl still, she had married her classmate, with whom she had now been living for the past twelve years.

Twelve years is an interesting period. It marks the cycle of Jupiter when many processes undergo a stage either of completion or transformation. People often get divorced after twelve years, meet someone new, take on a new job or start their own business.

Indira's husband adored her and despite his high position, gave her the upper hand.

Although strict and serious at work, she completely transformed in the company of friends where she became responsive, cheerful and charming. Everyone loved her. Most importantly, Sergey could see that she was real, lively and passionate, the kind of woman who could make any man happy. He felt somehow that Indira was his woman. Moreover, without the slightest cause for hope, he was absolutely convinced that he would one day marry her.

Many talented people are mystics by nature and have a developed intuition, the so-called sixth sense. They are able to foresee many situations in life and are always one step ahead of everyone else. Perhaps this is the key reason for their luck and success.

At this point, Sergey could sense that not everything was going smoothly in Indira's magnificent family. The problem was that she was too indulged. Her husband was too soft, intelligent and boring. Sergey could see that the woman in her slept and that the feelings she had for her husband was more like those of a sister for a brother, nothing more. He knew that when the passion in her was awakened, she would be unstoppable. And he knew what he was doing when he began to give her his attention. It was no petty love affair, of which there might be several in a man's life, but a great love that could last a lifetime. He tried to test his feelings for her and even spent time with other women but nothing came close.

The decision matured in him when Indira did not come to the hospital for a long time because both her children were ill, one after the other. Sergey decided to act decisively and openly, realising that there was simply no other way.

When she finally returned to work, Sergey suddenly realised that there was hope. The sparkle in her eyes and her smile spoke louder than any words. There was that special exciting-sparky energy between them that always marks the initial stages of love.

Their romance did not begin easily. Sergey, who was madly in love declared his feelings openly while the young woman looked back at him with her beautiful dark-brown eyes and asked him to stop.

During this period, he appeared in my office and told me how exactly what was predicted had come about. In his horoscope, there were all the indications of marriage and a trip in the near future that would turn out to be life-changing.

"Well, that's highly unlikely," he laughed. "She's not going to go anywhere with me."

But God's ways are inscrutable, and a month later Indira was sent on an internship to Moscow. She left, and a day later, Sergey followed her. When he appeared at her room dressed solemnly in white, that was it. It was spring and they walked the streets of Moscow talking about anything and everything and they were happy. Neither said a word about the future — both understood the complexity of the situation and preferred not to discuss it.

Shortly before the trip to Moscow, Indira had a dream, which a grandmother-sorceress helped her to interpret. It was one of those great prophetic dreams when many years ahead are compressed into symbolic form.

She saw herself walking along a wide village road wearing black shoes that were a little bit tight. There were a pair of light sandals on the side of the road, and so kicking off her black shoes, Indira put the sandals on and carried on her way. Amazingly, the sandals were the perfect fit, the sun was shining, and she felt carefree and happy. Suddenly, a luxurious car stopped nearby, a door opened, and Indira found herself sitting on a soft comfortable seat. Everything was fine except for the burden of an old handbag. Indira took from the bag her children's birth certificates, which for some reason turned out to be three, and threw the bag onto the side of the road.

Having listened to Indira, the grandmother said, 'The road means that you will leave here soon. A change of shoes indicates big change involving a new person with blond hair; the expensive car symbolises that you will live well, and the three certificates mean that you will have another child'.

We don't always pay attention to our dreams, sadly. Dreams are an important part of our life. They give us access to valuable information, and can sometimes help us to better understand our own desires. The sages of antiquity had the saying, 'If the gods love a person, they will reveal to them their intentions in a dream.' Sometimes dreams can warn us of trouble and are a direct indication of what is about to happen.

The grandmother's dream interpretation was very accurate. All that could be added is that subconsciously Indira was actively looking for change — her old shoes pinched and the colour black could be an indication of a measured but, nonetheless, not very joyful life. The light-coloured sandals symbolised the desire for happiness, light and freedom, something which Indira's soul had long been ready to allow into her life.

But our rational mind and our deepest desires often contradict each other and in order to find an acceptable balance between the two, we often deceive ourselves over our true motives. We cleverly exclude from the conscious mind all that runs counter to our notions of morality or that fails to correspond to convention. And so Indira chose to interpret the dream in her own style — her husband would receive a position in St. Petersburg and a move would be quite possible. There was nothing surprising in the birth of a third child as in Central Asian families it is quite usual for there to be a large number of children. A new man, to say nothing of one with blond hair, did not fit into her plan at all. Yes, she liked Sergey, but to let her entire life fall apart on his account? No, that could never be. And anyway, what would he, a handsome, clever, pragmatic young man want with a married woman and one with two children at that?

Men often paid her attention. She was used to it. But the situation with Sergey was different. Although fragile-looking and feminine she had a strong character and, one way or another, managed to subjugate most people to her will. Raised in a strict, Muslim family with strong traditions, she had remained free and independent. She had made her own decision about her profession, her marriage and she was making her own way in life. She observed Sergey, day after day, and saw how he worked, managing a large team of people who trusted him, and like any real woman, she could not help but give credit where credit was due. He was stronger than she was. He evoked the desire to follow his lead. He was one of those people who 'took care of things'.

'Now that's a real man. His wife is going to be a very lucky woman,' she sometimes thought and could not help being a tiny bit envious. Inexperienced in the games of love, she did not notice how Sergey was becoming an ever greater part of her life. True love is contagious, and Indira found she could not let a single day go by without seeing those attentive grey-blue eyes and without hearing that deep, low, velvety voice that seemed to excite her. When Sergey declared his love, she was genuinely happy.

It turned out that the observant Sergey was right. Indira's relationship with her husband was steady and fraternal but it had never been about a magical attraction or the kind of mysterious passion that nothing can contain.

Indira did not yet know herself well enough to suspect what she might be capable of if someone were to awaken all that within her. Nonetheless, she sensed that the connection with Sergey was dangerous, and so although she welcomed his love into her soul, she did not want to let him into her life. She left for Moscow with the vague hope that everything would somehow resolve itself.

Sergei's arrival in Moscow only seemed unexpected on the surface of things. In reality everything unfolded in a surprisingly logical manner. Once people are out of their familiar environment, they can temporarily forget about morality surprisingly quickly and follow their heart. And when an event is destined to happen, fate itself will create the necessary conditions.

After they both returned home, the lovers continued to see each other but, as before, they did not talk about the future. Indira could imagine what great sorrow she would bring to her large family, and Sergei did not want to push things and cause her problems.

However, there is always a 'do-gooder' to be found, willing to intervene in someone else's life in order to 'sort it out'. That is what happened in Indira's case. The 'well-wishers' turned up and Indira's husband found out about the affair. To give him credit, the husband talked calmly to his wife about it all and she was as honest with him as she could be.

"All sorts of things happen in life. Let's forget about all this and I'll take you away to St.Petersburg. There, we can start a new life and you'll forget about him. We have two children."

"I can't. I can't live without him. I love him."

"And what about him? Does he love you? Will he marry you?"

"I think so, yes."

"Well, I would not be so sure if I were you. Not every man is jumping at the bit to bring up someone else's children."

It is hard to believe but this calm, sensible woman, brought up in the Eastern traditions, was ready to drop everything and take a leap into the unknown with her Russian lover. Nothing could stop her, not the huge, family scandal, which would inevitably take place, nor the prospect of being judged by her friends, colleagues and acquaintances.

For a woman who has been brought up in a traditional Muslim family, to take up and leave her husband just like that is unthinkable, impossible even. To say nothing of leaving a good, high-ranking husband who adored her. And leave him for whom? For a man of a different nationality, faith and uncertain future? The scandal would affect her parents, her relatives and their entire social circle.

In an attempt to save his family, Indira's husband met with his wife's lover. Sergey was ready. He had been waiting for the situation to resolve itself for a long time and was keen for this to come about sooner rather than later.

The conversation was short, tough and frank.

"How many years have you been in love with Indira?"

"Two."

"I have loved her my whole life. Stay away from her. I'm taking her away to St. Petersburg and she'll forget all about you."

"That's for Indira to decide. I'll marry her tomorrow if she'll have me."

"I think she has already made her decision... Remember this. If she is happy with you, I won't stand in her way. But I'll be watching you. And I'll make sure that she and the children never want for anything."

"You don't need to worry on that account."

And that was it. Neither spoke ever again. As it was impossible for Indira and Sergey to live together in their home town, they took the children and moved to Moscow, where their love first began. You could say that they 'leaped empty-handed into the void'.

A year later their son was born. At first, they lived in a shared apartment and life was hard but Sergey established himself very quickly and exactly ten years after this story began, he had become a successful, wealthy businessman. Their children received an excellent upbringing and education and they had a wonderful home.

I asked Sergey once why he had never doubted the sanity of what he was doing. He replied, 'it was the most sane thing I've ever done in my life! I just realised that I would never be happy without her, and would never achieve anything without her. No-one wants someone who is unhappy, not least themselves, right?'

Great words indeed! In a way, they are a kind of comprehensive answer to all our questions. It's true. No-one wants to be around people who are unhappy. But first you have to understand what makes you happy and then be unafraid to take the road towards achieving it.

Many people live in constant expectation of future happiness, and live their life as if it were a prelude to something else, more important. They put everything off for another day and forget that life is lived in the here and now, that every moment in life is unique. Every moment disappears into the past forever and can never be returned.

Others make their own path and push forward relying on their strengths and capabilities; for people like this, every minute of every day has significance. Sergey was one of these people. Happiness is what he wanted and happiness is what he found.

Signs

It is interesting to note that we can learn about the future from almost anything if we are attentive to what is going on around us. Reading signs is one way predicting the future. All peoples have a set of signs which they take to symbolise the success or failure of a future undertaking. Empty buckets, black cats and yellow flowers symbolise a negative time flow and obstacles to a person's plans and worldly affairs. It is interesting that Bulgakov's Margarita[5] was walking down the street carrying yellow flowers, a symbol of her loneliness, and then after meeting the Master, threw them away.

Pregnant women, weddings, red roses and 'lucky numbers' signal a positive time flow, a kind of 'green light' to our plans and dreams. All sorts of things can serve as a sign. The most important thing is to understand what kind of time flow you are currently in.

I was going to an important interview once and naturally, I was very nervous. I did not know whether I could hold my own with the competition. And then I saw a poster advert displaying the word 'victory' and realised that everything would go well, as in fact, it did.

I was telling a friend once about my rather ambitious plans for the future. 'It won't work out,' she said with scepticism. And then the host of the TV program, which was on in the background, said solemnly,

---

[5] Margarita is the main female character in Mikhail Bulgakov's 'The Master And Margarita'.

'You will succeed!' Even my very materialistic friend understood that this was a sign and said, 'there you have your answer. You will be successful.'

One of my clients once told me that she determined the quality of her relationship with the man she loved by reading advertisements outside. Her lover was in a very unhappy marriage but, nonetheless, did not intend to divorce his wife. They had a young child and divorce would have meant being separated from the child. Nevertheless, the love between my client and this man was real, and both suffered terribly and argued often.

One day, my client saw a large poster depicting a man sitting between two women. On that same day, her lover told her that his wife was an important part of his life and that he did not intend to leave her. And all the time that this poster caught her eye here and there in the town, the situation did not change. Then, one day she noticed a new advert had been put up where the old one used to be showing two people lost in a kiss and displaying the word 'faith'. At that time, their relationship was improving and their love was growing stronger. My client started paying attention to the adverts she saw and found that they clearly predicted all the changes she experienced in the relationship. And just after a new motif appeared in the poster illustration - a man giving a woman a ring, - the man told my client that his wife was willing to let him have custody of their child and he offered her then his hand and heart. The world was speaking to her and she understood its language.

Almost anything can be used for divination. In the East, they read a person's palm or use stones, flour, coffee and tea. In the West, people use standard playing cards, runes and the Tarot. What matters is not the system, so much as the diviner's personality and their ability to penetrate to the very essence of things.

All cultures have used astrology. It is the oldest and probably the most perfect divination system in existence. But it requires immense knowledge and long, thorough training to learn. Signs can help people navigate the flow of time independently and determine the direction it will take in the future. All changes in life are accompanied by corresponding signs of fate. You just have to be able to notice them and interpret them correctly. Sometimes, however, this is very difficult to do.

ROMAN

One of the most difficult life stories that I encountered during my time as a practicing astrologer was accompanied by what appeared to be completely innocent signs, which it turned out later, I had misinterpreted.

Being a well-known astrologer in my native republic of Kyrgyzstan, I often met people working in parallel professions. Once, my husband (a doctor and astrologer practicing various kinds of energy work) and I were introduced to a famous fortune-teller. She was an unusual, bright, witty and lively woman albeit a little odd. Her name was Marina, Mara for short. She was a coffee-cup fortune-teller and claimed to be able to remove a curse and heal, too. Despite her outright immodesty, she was extraordinarily charming. Being Georgian with a pleasantly rough-throaty voice and Caucasian accent only added to her charm.

She divined very well as long as she had no personal attachment to the outcome. But if she wanted something, then she would use all the tools at her disposal, divination, intrigue, and outright insidious slander to achieve it. However, all this only became clear much later on. At the dawn of our acquaintance, she gave the impression of being a charming, cheerful, witty individual.

All sorts of interesting people would gather at Marina's home and on one warm Saturday evening, my husband and I were passing and decided to pop in and see her. As always, there were people in the living room and my weekly program 'Astrological Forecast' was showing on TV. A handsome, young blond who was sitting in an armchair turned around, recognised me and introduced himself as Roman. He had already met my husband previously and they quickly got chatting. It was not clear what he was doing at Marina's house but we presumed he was a client who had just become a good friend of the hostess. He had brought her a video of the movie 'Ghost' — that season's hit. We all watched the film together and everyone afterwards remarked upon how similar Roman was to the hero in the film, 'Sam'. And with characteristic spontaneity, Mara nicknamed Roman 'Sam'. The name stuck and soon everyone started to call him Sam.

It has to be said that Marina herself was surprisingly reminiscent of the fortuneteller played in the film by Whoopi Goldberg. (For anyone who has not watched this beautiful, innocent, touching film, the main character, Sam, was killed and for some time remained on Earth as a ghost. He revenged his killer and saved his girlfriend, Molly, whom he was madly in love with and had intended to marry.)

The back story to Roman's visit to the 'coffee cup' fortune-teller was pretty standard. He was in love with a married woman, the mother of two children, and could not bear to live without her. Seeing how deep the lad's affection for her was, the woman involved took him for granted; she would fail to turn up on dates and then not bother to call and, what is more, she seemed to take some kind of sadistic pleasure in it all. She was married to a handsome, wealthy Tajik[6], who humiliated her and had a handful of mistresses, which he made no attempt to hide.

The situation was complicated by the fact that she was Russian and his Tajik relatives always treated her with disdain. They saw her as nothing more than a servant. The reason she was playing this kind of role in the relationship with her lover was because she had learned that if you do not 'crush' a man, he will definitely 'crush' you.

Roman came to Marina in the hope of finding some explanation for his strange attachment to this woman (who for the sake of this story we'll call Nina). The lonely, temperamental Marina fell instantly in love with this handsome, intelligent, vulnerable young man and was quick to instil in him the idea that the woman he loved was a witch who was casting an insidious spell over him. She described the process of enchantment in great detail and insinuatingly promised him that it would all come to an end very soon, by which time 'Sam' would find a new love (of course, she was talking about herself).

The unsuspecting young man believed all her fairy-tales. It is always easier to put one's own suffering down to supernatural forces than to accept the reality of unrequited love. How often are abandoned women comforted by the firm assumption that their rival has in fact only 'bewitched' the object of their passion rather than inspired his love. To admit that one's rival is the better woman is painful and humiliating. It is so much easier to believe that one's former love has simply 'come under a spell'. Many fortune-tellers exploit this psychological approach, and it is always 'a hit'.

---

[6] Ethnic group native to Afghanistan, Tajikistan, and Uzbekistan

Marina was no exception. She knew very well what she was doing when she convinced Roman that his situation was a case of well-practised witchcraft and had nothing to do with love at all. He would disappear for days at Marina's house, where they performed magical rites together aimed at 'liberating' him from the hold of his deceitful lover.

One of the conditions of the divination service was that Roman should not see his lover at all and this had a positive affect. Seeing that her lover was no longer showing any initiative, Nina became concerned. She started calling him herself but he refused to see her and became distant.

Now the boot was on the other foot. Having been used to playing the tyrant, Nina instantly switched to the role of abandoned victim. This often happens with people who do not know how to love and so indulge in psychological game-playing instead. When the situation allowed it, she played the role of 'executioner', and when it did not, she instantly transformed into the role of victim. Such are the 'sado-maso' swings on which relationships are often based.

The abandoned mistress could not understand what was happening at first but having carried out some research, she quickly got a handle on the situation, which was quickly getting uglier. Roman-Sam had meanwhile dropped out his research programme, started drinking and spent days at a time with Marina. He genuinely considered her to be a friend. It never even occurred to him that the fortune-teller might want something completely different from him.

It was unbearable to watch and somehow I managed to intervene on account of my relationship with Marina.

"What are you doing? Surely you can see that this guy will never be yours? I can see what's driving you, and whatever comedy you're trying to pull off here, it won't work."

"Why should I be alone? She has a husband. Let her spend time with him!"

"It's nothing to do with you. Leave the lad alone."

"Don't stick your nose into my business. I'll deal with it myself. Don't interfere, please!"

Marina was very angry and with that our connection came to an end. I had no regrets, however, as her constant intrigue, cunning and 'witchy' manipulations as they became apparent repulsed me.

It was impossible to ignore what was happening and eventually, I ended up having to get involved as Nina herself came to see me, the woman who had been accused of black magic and decisively christened a witch. In front of me sat a pretty, bright, sexy 32-year-old woman. She had a great haircut, a beautiful athletic figure and dark, expressive eyes. She reminded me of someone. Who was it? Why, here was another character from the movie 'Ghost', Sam's lover Molly, who was so brilliantly played by Demi Moore! But whereas Roman-Sam was clearly more handsome and more expressive than the Sam in the film, his girlfriend was somehow less refined, and less expressive that the famous actress.

I felt uneasy catching myself involuntarily comparing Nina to the famous American actress. Why the similarity? Why had these three characters come together? Nina had come to me as a straight forward client, although we had mutual acquaintances and we had met somewhere before. Her chart eloquently spoke of problems in her personal life - a difficult marriage, which would soon end in a divorce, then a very difficult period, moving abroad, breaking up with her lover and three years later, another marriage which would probably be lasting. Our conversation took place at the end of April. The divorce was indicated as likely to take place in September of the same year, and her move abroad, one year after that.

Despite all the seriousness of the forecast, Nina did not seem to be too affected by the information. The only thing that really interested her was the current relationship with her lover.

The forecast was as follows: they would soon make up but, nonetheless, the connection was unlikely to last long. Two eclipses that would affect the client's Mars were clear indication of a relationship crisis and subsequent break-up. Within all this, the only words that Nina seemed to hear were 'soon make up'. This was clearly of much greater importance to her than the subsequent separation or emigration.

"I can't leave my husband. He's a Tajik and we have two sons. In eastern families, it is not custom for the children to stay with the mother, especially boys. He will never be the one to leave. Our life suits him as it is - family, children and complete freedom. He never lets a pretty 'skirt' pass him by. He's rich, good-looking and all doors are always open to him. I was madly in love with him, converted to Islam for his sake and we had a Muslim wedding. But I've lost all feeling for him after years of humiliation, fear, beatings and betrayal. Roman is the only man who has ever treated me with love. He is the first lover I have had in fourteen years of married life."

I knew she was lying. Roman was not her first. Her chart clearly indicated that she had a lover three years earlier. But that was not my concern. And then she started to cry and her face became more beautiful. The hardness had gone and in its place was a touching, defenceless, soft femininity.

"Please help me! I know that you are in contact with him. I'm being slandered. It's that crazy Marina. I called him, and you know what he said: 'Hang up! The full moon won't help you, witch!'"

Yes, Marina had seriously messed with the young man's head and things could not go on as they were. The conversation with Sam, which is what everyone called Roman now, took place the following day. It happened of its own accord and not through me but through my husband.

Sam popped into the office in the morning when I was not there. He was very upset and asked my husband what he thought about the situation. My husband explained to him what was really going on and revealed the true intentions of the 'coffee cup' fortune-teller.

"I've been such a fool! How could I have been so drawn in. It was all so obvious!"

Roman called Nina there and then. They agreed on a reconciliation and were happy. For a while, their happiness was so genuine and sincere that I began to doubt the astrological forecast I had made. At one point, they came to see us at the office and all they talked about was

Marina and the entire 'magic saga'. As the saying goes, 'they were united in their enmity against her.'

Watching how their relationship was transforming with each passing day, it became clear that what this couple needed in order to continue growing together was a common enemy. Without it, they would quickly become bored of each other. And since the theme of Marina could not last forever, they would need a fresh enemy. I began to suspect that quite soon, the enemy might be me or both my husband and I.

Any union between a man and a woman has to have a goal. Without it, the relationship will pale and gradually fade to nothing. The goal can be something obvious and constructive, for example, goals in the marriage between an actress and a director or a teacher and student. Many couples bring up children together and enthusiastically overcome the difficulties life throws at them.

Things get a bit more complex when the spiritual level of both partners (or lovers) is relatively low. In this case, they might take pleasure in a joint struggle against relatives or other enemy, which distracts them from complaints they might have against each other and makes their life much more interesting. However, once one goal has been achieved, for example, the children have grown up or the relatives have left them alone, the couple is faced with the difficult situation of having to find a new goal or face the reality of separating. Not many couples are successful in finding a substitute for what has been the meaning of their existence for so long and often it is this that leads to serious problems in the relationship.

Roman gradually became interested in astrology. He would come to the office early in the morning, spent hours reading books and casting horoscopes and he made good progress. My husband was the one who had been teaching him astrology and he was the first to voice what had long been obvious but left unsaid.

"I suspect they'll separate and your forecast will prove accurate. They are very different people. All they have is sex and that doesn't get you far in love." Moreover, their connection was rooted in pain and suffering from the very beginning. One of them absolutely had to be 'persecuting' the other. Without it the dynamic in their relationship was boring and bland. Nina was the one who instigated this tradition between them, as she was convinced that it was the easiest way of controlling the man she loved. She was already familiar with the role of 'victim' and so in the relationship with her lover was determined to be the 'persecutor'. However, the interference of her rival Marina had broken the stereotype and now there was more equality in their relationship. Nina was full of fear. She was not used to having stable happiness in her life and was constantly afraid of being abandoned. Slowly but surely, she was returning to the more familiar role of 'victim'.

People who have spent a long time involved in unhealthy codependent relationships are not usually capable of building normal, healthy relationships. They only understand two role types, the 'victim' and the 'executioner'. And when the role of 'executioner' turned out not to be working, Nina meekly resumed the more familiar role of 'victim'. She began to excessively indulge Roman, looking after him like a nanny. She was often jealous, and did all sorts of thing to spoil their love that were not at all necessary.

Mutually dependent relationships are dangerous both for the 'victim' and the victim's 'persecutor', above all because neither participant in the game is capable of stopping in time. The 'victim' believes that the more they put up with, the greater their chances of changing the 'persecutor's' behaviour, always thinking that each step on the path to humiliation will be the last. The road to hell is indeed lined with good intentions. The tormentor is always looking for increasingly sophisticated ways to strengthen their influence over the 'victim' thereby adding intensity to the emotions they feel.

We are not talking about physical torture here, the kind so vividly described by the notorious Marquis de Sade. It is more the kind of thing that starts with little jabs, for example, when one of the partners suddenly stops answering the other's calls and temporarily drops off the planet. Or it might take the form of supposedly innocent games, such as when one partner deliberately does not call when they say they are going to. The other partner feels tormented, not understanding what is going on, and they begin to take the initiative all the time being faced with the inconsistent behaviour of the object of their passion. As times goes on, the games intensify: the 'persecutor' gets into a groove and begins to play the role of 'heart-breaker', and the victim experiences pangs of jealousy. There are endless examples of this kind of behaviour and at the root of them all is the desire of one partner to manipulate the other.

Relationships like this always come to a difficult end. The day comes when the 'victim' has finally given their last and is totally drained. At this point, the 'persecutor' looses all interest in them and starts playing the same game with another, so-called 'fresher' partner.

The abandoned 'victim' is left in an extremely difficult situation; energetically robbed, trampled upon, their psyche damaged, there is no longer any room for a significant other in their life or for the experience of happy, positive emotions. It can often take the help of a good psychotherapist and for a lot of time to pass before the 'victim' can eventually forget what has happened and start over. They might be successful, they might not.

Things might also take a different course: the 'victim' one day realises that things cannot go on like this anymore and they simply leave the 'persecutor'. In this case, accustomed to syphoning off their partner's energy, the 'persecutor' suddenly finds themselves without a fuel supply and starts to try and get the rebellious partner back, failing to notice that they themselves have now ended up in the role of 'victim'. The roles shift - the 'executioner' becomes the 'victim' and the former 'victim' takes pleasure in assimilating the role of 'persecutor'.

Ultimately, this cruel game turns against both participants; step by step, they destroy any grain of love that might have been between them leaving only pain and disappointment. No-one should ever succumb to the desire to exploit their partner's weaknesses and any attempts at manipulation by a partner should be instantly nipped in the bud. Happiness can never be achieved by making a loved one suffer, at least whilst there is any spark of love in the relationship.

Any misunderstandings that inevitably arise in the early periods of a relationship should be sorted out straight away and for this to happen, both people have to learn to talk to one another. You might think this would be easy but many people find it difficult to discuss their problems with each other openly. The attitude of 'work it out yourself darling,' is one of the causes for bigger problems that ultimately lead two otherwise loving people to separate. When a woman takes this position, it is often down to the relationship stereotypes that exist in society: the woman should not be the one to take the initiative, and she should not take the first step towards someone she likes. And no matter how much people talk about the emancipation women, a woman's key principle remains passive perception. This is quite natural and understandable.

If the man takes a passive position, then things can lead to serious upheaval because it fundamentally goes against nature's principles. The man is the stronger, and this gives him the right to be the first to approach a woman when problems arise. Experience shows that the union between a couple is more harmonious and lasting when the man takes the lead and is the first to initiate reconciliation. This is especially important in the early stages of a relationship, when love is experiencing its spring and is still unstable and constantly fluctuating like 'an April's day, volatile and unfaithful.'

In Nina's case, she the one who tried to keep the relationship going and she did everything she could to keep Roman close to her. She was the one who initiated all the dates they went on and she never let any opportunity pass to spend time with him. In addition to all this, she read up on 'women's little tricks', the kind published in popular women's magazines, which supposedly can 'tie' a man to a woman, and she actively put them into practice.

As far as these 'tricks' are concerned, I have always thought they were written by people who have absolutely no understanding of love whatsoever. In reality, there is no connection stronger than the inner union between two people. And no emotion is more capricious or unpredictable than love.

Naive attempts to reduce relationships to something that can be managed by adopting more 'interesting' positions during sex or controlled by the ingenious manipulation of a partner are doomed to failure from the very beginning. If two people need each other and feel good together, they will find a common language in everything. Once the internal connection is lost, there is nothing that can be done and any attempts at this stage to save the relationship are equivalent to trying to resurrect the dead with a touch of blusher.

Roman was a talented biologist and academic. He carried out complex research, studied with enthusiasm and was planning to take part in the Soros competition. He cast his own horoscope, made forecasts for every day, and watched enthusiastically as they were fulfilled. He once asked me once whether I thought he would receive a Soros grant, and the answer from the horoscope was unequivocal — yes, he would. His passion for astrology was becoming more serious every day, which only increased the distance between him and Nina. She understood this and the image of the enemy was formed. It was indeed my husband and I and more myself than my husband.

And for no apparent reason, my relationship with this couple gradually deteriorated until it became nonexistent. The summer came and went. In the autumn, Nina took a decisive step and left her husband taking her two children with her. Perhaps she hoped that this step would serve as an ultimatum and force her lover to make a decision. But this did not happen. On the contrary, their relationship became much worse. Roman did not want to get married. He was already dreaming of America and making his own plans for the future, which did not include Nina.

And then a third party in the future drama appeared in my office — Nina's husband, a tall, thin, handsome Tajik called Rahim. He came with a question about his business affairs as he had transferred most of his funds to a certain lady, who promised to help him acquire a sizeable loan. The forecast was disappointing — the lady was most likely a swindler, and he would not receive the loan or get his own money back. It was unpleasant news to have to hear. Then my dismayed client asked another question: why did his wife leave and was there someone else? Only then did I understand who I was dealing with.

Usually, during a consultation, you only look at the client's date of birth. The client's name and surname are not significant to the chart and may not be known at all. That is what happened on this occasion. I worked with the details of the client's birth without paying attention to the name, and anyway, there is more than one Rahim in the world! It was when he gave me his wife's details that I understood who he was. It was impossible to answer him honestly, and I found myself in the kind of difficult situation that anyone in my profession could find themselves in, when talking about people they know.

"It may be that you yourself are to blame for the divorce. You love women too much."

"Who doesn't?" laughed my client.

Women found him very attractive. Of that there was no doubt. He was smart, sharp and very charming.

Suddenly, though, he frowned, his face darkened and his expression changed. What was that? Could he really be like the killer in the movie 'Ghost'? There was a similarity, although Rahim was much more good-looking, more interesting, intelligent and cultured than the character in the film. When he was in a good mood, there was no similarity at all but in moments of anger, the same tough features of Sam's killer came through clearly in my client's face. In this moment, he was getting more and more annoyed.

"She won't manage without me. The eldest son has already left her to come back and live with me. She has learned how to make money, but what of it? I will never let her have the children. And I don't totally believe in astrology or your forecast. The logic of life would suggest the opposite, at least for now."

While he was ranting, I recalled the film and could not understand why there should be such a striking similarity between my friends and the heroes of the famous film. Many actors are superstitious and believe that what you act out in a film, you will experience in life. Some refuse to play in scenes where they are killed or die. Recently, our beloved Russian prima donna Alla Pugacheva said, "I sing a song, and its plot instantly plays out in my life."

Why is this? Maybe because the strong emotional tension that an artist experiences during the performance of a song or role sends a powerful message into the future, and acquires form in accordance to the enacted cliche. Or maybe it is because a person involuntarily attracts those situations that are most consistent with their internal state. It is not surprising that many directors can only see one actor in a role and will not accept anyone else. Many actors say, that they are always playing themselves. On the other hand, an actor can find themselves in a film plot, which matches their future fate. We cannot know how it happens, just as we cannot know where lies the cause and where lies the effect.

In the situation that I was dealing with, no one was acting; they were just all incredibly similar to the heroes in the film. Why? What was it all about? There was no definitive answer but one thing was clear — it could not bode well.

Unfortunately, the forecast proved accurate and the strange client returned to my office. This time, his self-confidence was diminished — he had lost his money and did not receive the loan either. In addition, his wife had not returned to him, and their youngest son was dead set against living with his father.

"What will happen next?" Rahim asked anxiously.

"Very soon you will meet an old friend. He will help you get another loan but it is very important that you use the money well."

"What old friend? You don't know his name do you?" and he laughed.

"No, I can't tell you his name but he is much older than you and you have known him for a long time."

"And what about my wife? To tell you the truth, things aren't the same without her. Over these past fourteen years, I've got used to her and did not treat her badly at all. I earned the money, protected her from my relatives and took care of her and the children. Yes, I had affairs but who doesn't?"

Who could argue with logic like that or indeed his unshakable Central Asian confidence that a man may permit himself everything and a woman, nothing. Many men have the same opinion without for a moment considering the fact that while they are spending time with other people's wives, another man may be having just as much fun with their own.

"I'm such a fool. I taught her how to make money and even gave her the startup capital. That's why she's so brave now. But nothing will come of it and she'll come back to me. It's been four months since she left though. Has she met someone else or not? No, she can't have. She loves me and is just being difficult. She's decided to teach me a lesson."

The situation was clear. He wanted his wife back, and she, in love with Roman as she was, did not want to go back to him and cherished hopes of a marriage with her new love.

Yet Roman continued to distance himself from Nina, distracted by his plans for a life abroad and his interest in astrology. He had won the grant he applied for and was already preparing for the trip. I hardly ever saw him. He came to the office early in the morning, studied astrology and left before I arrived. I had felt the couple's hostility towards me and was glad that they were leaving me alone.

And suddenly what was bound to happen finally took place. The lovers had a conflict: Nina accused Roma of making plans to move to America without taking her into account. He replied sharply that he had never intended to marry her anyway. A split seemed inevitable and then Nina appeared at the office again. She genuinely could not understand what Sam's problem was (she, like everyone else, she had started Roman 'Sam').

"You're very different people, Nina. You don't want to do what he wants to do and now he has nothing to say to you any more."

"And so why before, when I was helping him with his business was he with me?" (Academics, even very talented ones, receive incredibly little in our country, and Roman had a side interest in trade, which had Nina helped him with.) "Why, if we are so different, do I love him but he doesn't love me?"

"You always love him when he leaves you. That's the problem in your relationship. One only loves the other when they start to distance themselves. Or you need a common enemy in order to be together. Recently I've been the enemy, right?" Nina was silent. "Try not making any demands on him. Don't pressure him. Be patient and wait. Let go of the situation. And by the way, you ought to know that your husband has been here. He is worried about the children and is starting to have suspicions. Take precautions and be careful, otherwise your love story will end in tears."

"Looks like it's already over, anyway. I know Rahim came for a reading and it's a good thing that he came here. If he had gone to anyone else, they would have told him everything. By the way, when we were still living together, he was planning to visit Marina. But I told him he'd be better off coming to you. I was afraid back then that he would find out and so tried to turn him in your direction."

Nina's approach was very practical and very selfish. Her assumptions were accurate and my opinion was of little importance to her. She knew very well that I would not divulge her secret. She was a very assertive, pragmatic individual and this side of her nature repelled many, including Roman.

But what about me? How did I end up involved in this whole story? I know work relationships and friendships should never be confused but, nonetheless, everything seemed to happen quite naturally. There is a reason they say that the road to hell is lined with good intentions. It appeared that the whole saga was only just beginning.

Very soon after that, I saw Roman who was choosing from the astrological textbooks in our office. More out of female solidarity than anything else, I asked him what his intentions were towards Nina. He blushed and said that he did not see a future in the relationship.

"But you drew her away from her husband, why?"

"It was not like that at all. I told her that if the reason she was leaving him was because she could not bear living with him any longer, then that was one thing, but she should not leave him on my account."

"But you helped her pack up and move to her mother's when her husband was away. When a lover does that kind of thing, a woman is justified in feeling her hopes are encouraged."

"She simply asked me to help her move her things. By then she had already firmly decided she was not going to live with him any more. It was not like I would refuse to help her."

Roman clearly did not see that Nina had been pushing him. Sometimes men fail to understand even the simplest things: a woman asks a man for help in order to bring them closer together. I should not have got involved and should have stepped away from them all, especially since I had absolutely no right to read Roman the riot act. It was, in truth, nothing to do with me.

"When are you leaving for America?"

"In a week's time."

"For how long?"

"Three months."

"Well, good luck then."

Clearly, all Roman's thoughts were with America, and a lover, especially one with two children, was not part of the game plan. Before departing, Roman dotted all the 'i's' and crossed all the 't's'. For Nina, it was all over.

In the meanwhile, the role of the third suffering party, the abandoned husband, noticeably intensified. He tried as hard as he could to get his wife back but she stood firm and was adamant that she would not go back to him. And at that point, this self-confident, impudent character changed. No amount of feigned bravado could hide his pain, loneliness and suffering. After six months of single life, he had come to the realisation that he loved his wife and could only depart on his bachelor voyages with a light heart if she was quietly waiting for him at home. His eldest son, the good-looking 14-year-old, also missed his mother very much but bravely tried to support his father. Despite being loyal to his Dad, the boy was in fact deeply distressed at being separated from his mother and brother. He dropped out of school and lounged about for days on end.

Rahim did in fact gain the support of an old friend and the promised loan. He began to believe in the miraculous power of astrology and after that came in to see me quite often.

It is worth pointing out that contrary to what some might think, many influential people consult astrologers and clairvoyants, and sometimes have their own trusted seer to whom they regularly turn. This is rarely spoken of publicly. Quite the opposite in fact, it tends to be carefully hidden. Why this should be the case it is not clear, after all, astrology provides a valuable source of information, nothing more. Moreover, throughout history, those in the highest positions of power have made use of astrology.

Many high-ranking individuals came to me at that time and working with them was not always easy. Sometimes they only hear what they want to hear and not what you actually say. And they only respond to the positive information, whereas the negative seems somehow never to reach their high-ranking ears. There are others though, more refined, thoughtful types, whose tendency is to check the things they are told and seem always to land on their feet.

Roman left for America. Nina suffered and immersed herself in her work. Her husband humbly sought her forgiveness, his pride long forgotten. I finally understood the full extent of his despair when he came to visit one day carrying a copy of the popular newspaper 'Oracle' which published advertisements for 'hereditary' magicians, clairvoyants and healers. He was interested in the advert of a certain Vladimir Vis, who gave a one hundred percent guarantee on the successful return of an estranged husband or wife as well as love-binding spells for lovers and mistresses. Nor was it a problem that he would have to fly from Central Asia to Moscow, which is not exactly next door. He asked me for my advice and my thoughts about it all. Naturally, the answer was negative. You can never turn someone's fate around in an opposite direction, and especially, those who advertise such things in the newspapers are incapable of doing so. I was absolutely convinced that this heroic venture would fail but the desperate husband left for Moscow anyway.

He returned a week later full of hope and expectation. With trepidation and awe, he showed me the set of needles that he had been instructed to hide somewhere on his obstinate wife's doorstep. In addition to them, he had brought back with him a love potion, which the eldest son was supposed to mix in one of his mother's drinks. It all looked very primitive but Rahim, whom the magician had convinced of the infallibility of these means, was full of enthusiasm and hope.

"You can't imagine the queues to see Vis!!! The women!! All dressed in diamonds and furs!" For Nina's husband this was proof enough and he set immediately about his 'military' actions. Burying needles under the gates of the house where his wife now lived turned out to be fairly straightforward, as was pouring the potion into her food and drink. All this was done without delay, and then all they could do was wait. The sorcerer promised that the love spell would take affect within a month to 40 days time and Rahim lived all that time in a state of joyful excitement.

However, time passed and absolutely nothing happened. A month passed, then 40 days passed but the 'bewitched' wife had no intention of returning to her husband. Not only that, she became obdurate and aggressive. Rahim had lost hope and decided to call Vis, who's answer was brief: 'Wait.' The whole thing turned out to be a complete waste of time and money and the abandoned husband found himself once again at a dead end.

Somehow during this tragicomic saga, we became friends, which seems to be the way of things, when one person trusts another with their secrets and is not afraid to be natural and open. In addition, the man in question had considerable charm and a great sense of humour, which he managed to hold onto even in this critical situation.

He was certain that since I was capable of drawing up forecasts, I was probably capable of much more besides, for example, bewitching people. It was impossible to convince him otherwise. First he offered me money. Then he went on about his feelings, the children and the 'holy' restoration of the family. In the end, he simply 'took offence' and disappeared.

During this time, Rahim's wife abandoned by her lover who had left for America, did something no-one would have expected. Motivated by extreme despair and the desire to be close to the man she loved, she made contact with a twenty-two-year-old Chechen who had relatives in America. It did not take the lad long to work out that Nina was rich, lonely and emotionally vulnerable, and that it would be not difficult to gain control over her.

An affair began, in which each party pursued their own interests; Nina wanted a connection with America and her new passion wanted her money. However, since both were young, attractive and lonely, the new romance seemed more than natural. Perhaps they enjoyed meeting up with each other. In any case, they did not try to hide their relationship and both appeared to be happy.

Then, Roman returned from America. His hopes at instantly setting up a successful new life in a foreign country turned out to be unrealistic. He began to realise that he was not in demand as he had no money, no contacts and was committed to a profession that required nurturing over a long period of time. What he needed was a dynamic, business-minded companion. As a couple, it would be easier and they could overcome the challenges much faster. He remembered his former lover and decided to give her a call. Maybe their long separation played a role, too, but he loved Nina, and feelings like that do not disappear overnight. Moreover, despite his charm and good looks, Roman was not at all a ladies man and there had been few women in his life. Study, work and mysticism — these were the sum total of his interests. Nina, however, told him honestly that she was getting married and planned to leave for America.

And here the strange and capricious wheel of love turned again and Roman sank into a depression. We learned of his problems completely by chance as he had stopped coming to our office at all. Many people said that he had changed a lot after returning from America, and not at all for the better. Now he was planning to emigrate. He wanted to get a job in America and managed to find one through Soros. He was supposed to leave the country in a year's time, while Nina and her new love would leave four months from the day.

Roman broke off his friendship with my husband. This seemed odd as aside from the fact that they used to get on very well, they had a certain mystical energy in common. Roman had never been baptised. He came from a friendly family of Old Believers[7], where all relatives were united by the grandfather, who could not have been less than 90 years old. In difficult moments in the family's life, all the relatives would gather at the grandfather's home, carry out magical rites and sing strange magical songs and incantations. Roman had told my husband about his past which had been a huge personal secret. And he had asked my husband to be his godfather and to give him a name that no-one else should know. And so, my husband was not only a friend but Roman's godfather.

---

[7] Eastern Orthodox Christians who maintain the liturgical and ritual practices of the Eastern Orthodox Church as they existed prior to the reforms of Patriarch Nikon of Moscow who served between 1652 and 1666.

My husband felt a great sense of responsibility as godfather and treated his godson with genuine warmth, respect and gentleness. In some ways they were similar. They were both talented, intelligent people, who were passionately mystical and likewise knowledgeable about such matters. Both had an interest in Tibetan practices. They learned to leave their bodies, knew how to work with dreams, and often agreed to meet each other in the dream space. Roman possessed the rare ability to learn in dreams. This was one of things that helped him in being awarded the Soros grant. One of the conditions for getting a job was fluency in the language, but Roman's level of English was poor. He genuinely learned English while he was sleeping!

Roman was quite a loner. He did not like to talk much about the things that interested him, and there was not nobody especially for him to tell. My husband was someone in whom he had placed great trust but the fact remained — their friendship ended after Roman's trip to America. Despite his tendency towards mysticism, Roman was quite a practical person. He knew the price of success and it was something towards which he consciously strove. I think he wanted to forget about Nina and the whole story connected with that relationship, and we happened to be part of it. Moreover, he felt uncomfortable with me after the last conversation we had before he left for America.

However, my husband had become attached to Roman and as his godfather felt a certain responsibility towards him. He tried to reconnect with Roman and called him on his birthday.

Roma's mother answered and having politely inquired who was calling, she said that Roma was not home although my husband could hear his voice from the far end of the room, and understood that Roman simply did not want to speak with him. After that, all communication between them ceased.

The whole story appeared to have reached an end, and yet it left me with a vague sense of anxiety. There did not seem to be any grounds for concern. All the forecasts I had made had been fulfilled. Nina and her Chechen had left for America and if rumours were true, Roman was set to follow in their footsteps. There was no sign of Rahim. It seemed that he had finally accepted the situation and let go of his wife who had escaped with the Chechen.

Six months passed, and we had practically forgotten about the whole affair, when we received a phone call out of the blue.

"You did not tell me the most important thing; my wife was having an affair with Roman, who happened to be someone you knew very well." The tone of Rahim's voice was harsh and unpleasantly domineering.

"That's not true. Who told you that?" I asked, confused. He mentioned Marina, the very same 'coffee cup' fortune-teller, who, of course, knew everything.

"Why told you that? It's all in the past now and anyway she's with someone different."

"Why could not you have told me the truth? I trusted you..." The tone of his voice changed to sorrowful and pleading.

"I can't talk about this over the phone. Come and see me at the office."

And so he came, his eyes blazing, his hands trembling, frantically clinging to a cigarette and dropping his lighter. He bent down and struggled to pick it up. I had never seen him like this before. He was like a boy who had just lost his first love. He was completely thrown by his wife's betrayal, the wife, whom he had barely noticed, whom he had cheated on constantly and who had now run away with another. Truly it is the case that, 'we never want what we have until it's gone.'

"She was seeing the lad for a couple of years. He's the reason we got divorced. I always knew there must have been something going on! A woman never leaves a man for nothing. There's always someone else involved. My God, and there was I constantly getting laid and never even suspected a thing!" He was quiet for a moment as if thinking it over and then continued.

"You knew everything and said nothing."

"Well, firstly, I did not know 'everything', and anyway, why would you trust Marina?" I made a feeble attempt to direct his anger away from Roman.

"I checked and all the information she gave me is correct. Lots of people knew and lots of people saw them together. But no-one said a word, imagine, not a word."

"And rightly so. Calm down. She has left and left with someone else completely. Let it go. There are some things that can't be changed. And anyway, you were cheating on her constantly. Did you really have any right to expect her fidelity?"

"That's different. I am a man. I earned the money and gave it to her. She was my wife and is the mother of my children. I would never have abandoned her or started another family. Nothing else really matters. She was the one who destroyed our family, not me and that young man is as much to blame as she is."

"Remember, he was much younger than her. It was her desire and her choice and now she is not even with him."

I could see that Rahim was looking for someone to blame just as I could see that he was out of control. We spent the next four hours like this. He smoked, paced the room trying to dig through all the details. I listened and said nothing. He needed to get it all off his chest. That was the most important thing. I cancelled all my clients and shut the office sensing that it would be dangerous to leave him alone in that state. When he finally quietened down, I managed to switch the topic of conversation to the son who lived with him, and the woman whom he had been dating for the past six months. She was young, beautiful, madly in love with Rahim and of course wanted to get married. But Rahim was a difficult man to marry. He was used to female charms and anyway, he was not in love with her. However surprising, he now compared every woman he ever met to his wife. And the more that time passed, the clearer he could imagine her. Even now, that he knew she was cheating on him, he dreamed of somehow returning everything to how it use to be. I could see that he was prepared to forgive her affair, to forgive her everything, if only she would come back to him from distant America.

"You know, I don't bear her a grudge. I would forgive her everything. But now, I'll never have the opportunity to tell her so. There are much more important things in life than infidelity, and although few people would understand, I would live with her again. I loved her and I still do. That's the most important thing."

At this point in our conversation he spoke extremely frankly and openly but fate does not always give a person the chance to start life over again.

"Maybe I should travel to America? Surely this Chechen guy will leave her, if he has not already." Rahim asked me to stay in contact with them. "It's hard for me and my son. Sometimes, you just need to talk so that you don't obsess about people judging you or laughing at you."

When our conversation finally came to an end it was late and we were both exhausted. He did not come back to the office after that.

Another five months passed and New Year was approaching. Roman was just about to leave for America forever. According to rumours, Nina had been tricked by her Chechen lover. He abandoned her, having taken all her money. She lived alone and was working hard. Rahim continued to manage his business but not particularly successfully. We did not see each other after that and the whole story appeared finally to have reached its conclusion.

There was a sudden roll of thunder. I popped into an Italian boutique, where Roman's sister worked and where I sometimes bought clothes. On this occasion, she was not there and the second shop assistant said, "there's been a tragedy in the family. Her brother was killed last night." Everything started to swim before my eyes and I saw a vivid image of the murder. Rahim instantly came to mind. I am no clairvoyant but on this occasion the image of the killers flashed before my eyes — there were three of them.

"Were there three of them?"

"So you already know? Yes, there were three of them. They broke in, tied up the parents and waited for him to come home."

I began to feel ill and sank into a chair. I had to go to the office and do something. I thought of my husband, who despite the breakdown in the relationship, was still attached to his godson, loved him, and was genuinely happy for him, his success and the forthcoming move to America.

I don't remember how I got to the office. All I remember was the dirty, slushy snow, and terribly heavy feelings of pain, loss and inevitability. When I arrived, my sister and my husband were there.

"Roma's been killed," I said. They stared at me in disbelief. My husband called his acquaintance who was a homicide detective. He said that no such case had been opened and that Roman's name did not appear in his records. There was hope. An hour later, the detective called back to tell us that our friend was in intensive care. He was seriously injured but he was alive. We did not sleep that night and prayed to God for his life. But that was not Roman's fate. He never regained consciousness and died towards evening that same day.

A week later, Rahim called and asked how things were as if nothing had happened. Without answering his question, I accused him of murder. There was a pause.

"People don't kill for things like that. It's just your astrological fantasies talking. What would I hope to gain? You know very well that my wife left for America long ago." After another short pause, he asked casually, "Who else knows of your suspicions? Have you talked to anyone else?"

"No," I replied, knowing very well what he meant. I was scared, not for myself but for my loved ones, my children, sister and husband. I sensed that Rahim was lying and that the killers were still free. I had no evidence other than my own unconfirmed sense of conviction. And who would ever take into account the intuition of an astrologer? The police and other organisations consult with astrologers and clairvoyants but they never advertise the fact. Moreover, they will go out of their way to deny any connections of the kind. Rahim knew this very well and added mockingly, "You're one step away from Ward No.6,[8]" and then he put the phone down on me.

Scenes from the movie 'Ghost' suddenly flashed before my eyes. Yes, Sam was killed but he took revenge on all his killers. Roman has been renamed Sam two years ago and now he was murdered! At what point did his fate become a foregone conclusion? Surely not then? And if the plot of the film were to duplicate further, then all those involved in the murder would be punished in one way or another, and what's more, punished by the victim.

Roman was buried. He was unrecognisable, his face deformed and swollen from a head wound. They said that on the day of the funeral,

---

[8] Ward No.6 - a short story by Anton Chekhov set in a provincial mental asylum.

Nina called from America. She did not know what had happened and asked Roman's mother to ask him to come to the phone.

"He's lying in a coffin," his mother answered her. According to the parents' account of events, at 6 p.m. on that fateful day, three young strangers burst into the apartment. They asked for Roman but he was not home. Then they sat the parents on the sofa and told them not to move.

"Your son is to blame and he will answer for everything."

"For what?"

They said something about huge sums of money and someone being ruined. The parents knew nothing and could not work out what it was all about. Roma returned two hours later. One of the guys went out into the corridor and hit him hard on the back of the head. Then they all rushed outside into the street. Covered in blood, Roman went into the bathroom, began washing his face and told his mother to call an ambulance.

By the time the ambulance came, he was unconscious. By the next evening, he was gone. The three lads were Russian. Rahim was not among them. I began to doubt that he was the culprit. And although many knew that Roma had been Nina's lover for about two years, no-one thought to suspect her ex-husband. After all, his unlucky wife had fled to America with a Chechen. What did Roman have to do with anything?

Everyone was talking about a sum of money from the Soros Foundation, saying that the killers had taken Roman's notebook in which he kept the telephone numbers of all his friends. And again, there was a strange resemblance to the film in which the killer stole a notebook.

Three days later, I noticed a grey, expensive-looking car parked not far from my home. We arrived home late at around 9-10 in the evening and the car was not far from the entrance. I could make out two lads I did not know sitting in the car and it might have been quite an ordinary occurrence if it were not for that same persistent sense of anxiety. I have been very tense for a long while and acknowledging the state I was in, I chose not to share my suspicions with my husband. He had gone through a lot recently, too, and I did not want to worry him unnecessarily.

The next day the scene repeated itself: at one o'clock in the morning, I heard a car drive up to the entrance. The lights in the house were already turned off and I looked out through the window. My heart was pounding with alarm. It was that same car. Not saying a word, I got up and turned on the light. My husband was surprised and asked me what I was doing. It was time to tell him about the mysterious car and my fears.

"It's probably just a coincidence," he said trying to reassure me.

We lived in an apartment on the ground floor and there were no railings outside the window or iron doors. I had never been afraid of being robbed. There was nothing to steal. Our entire wealth was in the books my mother had started collecting. After staying there for a while, the car eventually drove away. I started to calm down and turned off the light but could not sleep.

At four in the morning, I heard the familiar sound again. It was the same car. It was lit up by the streetlight and I could see two, heavily-built, short-haired men sitting inside. I was afraid. I knew what it could mean. I alone had guessed at the true reason for Roman's death. And although there was no evidence, my husband and I could pose a real threat to the killers. My fourteen-year-old son was asleep in the next room. I instinctively picked up the telephone but there was no dialling tone. The phone was not working. The room began to swim before my eyes. I jumped up and turned on the lights. 'I'll show you, we're not asleep!' And then I woke my husband. This time he was worried, too. 'What are we going to do? Sit and wait? The door's hanging on good-will alone. The slightest push and it will fly off the hinges. The phone's not working.' The neighbours? We could not reach them. The car was hovering right outside the entrance and anyone who left the building would be spotted instantly. My husband turned on all the lights and checked the phone again. There was still no dialling tone.

The men were sitting in the car but it appeared they had realised we weren't asleep and did not know what to do next. We sat there waiting for an excruciating hour by which time it began to get light and the car drove away. Someone had cut the telephone wire. At 9 a.m., exhausted, I called Rahim and told him that if anything happened to me or my family, everyone would learn the reason. He seemed seriously angered and offended by what I had said.

"If I had wanted to get rid of you, I would have done it in a different way. You need psychiatric help."

However, later that same day, I learned that he had left the city, leaving his son alone at the apartment. No-one saw him after that. He seemed to have disappeared forever. I will never know whether he was connected to this story or not but the strange car did not turn up outside our house again after that.

Meanwhile, strange, mystical things started happening to us. Three days after the funeral, Roman came to my sister, who was an exceptionally talented clairvoyant and could see the past and the future. As situations related to the distant future remained hidden from her, she did not work professionally but she helped me a lot in various situations that were difficult.

Their family went to bed early. Her husband got up every morning at five. That day, he had fallen asleep in the next room, and she was lying in bed thinking about Roma and about the whole saga. The dog, which had been lying calmly next to her suddenly whined and flew out of the room like a bullet from a gun. The air around her became cold and according to my sister, the cold pressed her to the bed so numbing her body that she could not move her arms or legs. Roman's head and shoulders appeared as if through a fog while the rest of his body was blurry, almost transparent. He spoke but the words sounded inside my sister's head as she telepathically perceived what he was saying.

"I need to talk to you. There's something I have to tell you."

"Leave me alone!" my sister yelled in fear. "Go away!"

"Listen," Roman said.

"No, I can't!" My sister could not speak she was so scared and the visions suddenly dissolved. A little while later, my husband started to see Roman in dreams just as he had during the time they were still friends. Roma told him of his life in the other world and of his new home where he was happy. My husband felt the death of his godson very deeply and was happy to see him, albeit in a dream. Unlike me, he was not convinced that Rahim was Roman's killer. As a philosopher and mystic, he had looked for the true cause of Roman's death but did not find it. What had Roma done, and why did his life come to an end at the age of 29?

At first, my husband was pleased of the opportunity to communicate with his friend in dreams but soon found that the process exhausted him. He lost a lot of weight very quickly, almost 10 kilograms. He became weak and lethargic. It was as if his life force was leaving him. Then, in a dream once, Roman took him by the shoulders and said, 'Do you want me to show you heaven?'

And with that they both rose quickly above the earth. My husband lost consciousness in his sleep and soon after that incident was seriously ill for a long time. It would seem, the living are not meant to keep contact with the world of the dead. It requires too great on output of energy, causing a person to become depleted as they slowly begin to waste away. That is what happened on this occasion and my husband's illness lasted for about three years.

Once, I participated in one of these dreams. I walked into our small astrology shop and saw Roman standing beside the books holding my husband's hand. I walked past them into another room and got the impression that they had not noticed me. The following morning, my husband told me that he had met with Roma in a dream again. They were in the shop and suddenly the door opened. I came in, walked past them and went into another room.

In these dreams, Roman did not say anything about his killers. They did not seem to be concerned about them. Just once, he appeared in an unusual distorted form with an elongated skull and bulging eyes, and there was an aspect of the demonic in his appearance. He kept on contacting the living and there was a reason for his proximity to Earth — revenge.

After this, I was certain that the killers would soon be caught as indeed they were. The breakthrough came as a matter of chance, via something fairly incidental. Either there was a quarrel in a restaurant and a group of pushy guys refused to give in to equally pushy representatives of the law, or they got involved in trying to protect some girls who had fallen into a 'Caucasian ambush' and were detained. One of the detainees was identified at the police station. He was surprisingly similar to a photo composite compiled by Roman's parents. The parents came in and recognised the men as their son's killers. They did not deny it and gave Rahim away, who by that time had disappeared from the city without trace. He had disappeared forever, at least, no-one ever saw him here again. This story ended exactly like the film plot in 'Ghost'.

Strangely, in all the time I was acquainted with Roman, I never once looked at his horoscope in the same way I had done with my other clients. We talked about his relationship with Nina, and I understood that until he reached the age of 29 he would not have a stable relationship with a woman, or get married. Seeing a tough connection between

Mars and Saturn in the area that rules love, I confidently predicted their separation and all sorts of upset around it. We talked about the Soros grant, the trip to America and his abilities in the sphere of the occult. After that, he worked a lot on his horoscope independently, literally by the day.

Once he spoke to my sister, and said, 'I have several unlucky days in a row in early January. What might that mean?' She replied, 'Take a look at the period after that.' Roman replied, 'After that, a journey's indicated.' Roman assumed it was connected to America but the journey to God can sometimes look the same in a chart as long-distance travel.

Once you start being friends with a person, it becomes impossible to predict their death. The mind simply cannot conceive of the idea that this same person whom you see every day might suddenly die. I was often asked about this afterwards: 'You knew he was going to die. Why didn't you warn him?'

'I did not know actually.' I would reply. 'All I saw was a difficult, negative period, that would be very painful and emotional, but at the time, I believed it would be a consequence of the loss of love and a deep emotional crisis.' I can say categorically, that I did not for a second imagine that Roman would die in early January at the hands of killers.

It should also be said that death can present itself in very different ways in a person's horoscope. If a person is destined to die in old age, quietly and peacefully, the death can present itself as a long journey to another, more comfortable place. This was how my grandmother died — a very calm, devout and kindly woman. At the age of 96 she started to go downhill. She did not eat for three days, and without experiencing torment or suffering, she passed over to the world.

A tragic, premature death can present itself in a chart as severe stress, disaster and emotional trauma. Here the tragic tendencies are more pronounced, and if they are duplicated across several astrological techniques, then one may assume that death is indicated. It is impossible to discuss such things with the client, however, because as one famous English astrologer said, 'they simply won't survive it.' Although many people ask, 'How long will I live?', it is better not to touch on the topic at all, except in cases of extreme necessity.

It is one of those things it is better not to know. It is still stressful to hear even if a person still has another sixty years ahead of them. It may not matter much now, but later on closer to the fateful year, it begins to weight on a person's mind and nothing good can come of that. I remember how afraid my mother was when she had to have an operation. She was a little over 70 years old at that time and was convinced she was going to die on the operating table. Trying to comfort her, I told her the alleged fateful year, which happened to be a long time after the date of the operation. At first, my mother was glad. She had never imagined that she would live so long. Now though, that year is approaching and the knowledge of it burdens her. It has certainly taught me a lesson. Some questions are better left unanswered.

Sometimes people leave when they have completed their main task in life or have begun to go downhill, or down the path that is least desirable for them. Deaths like this often take place around the ages of

27-29 or 37-40. In a horoscope this might present itself as a change of environment or a shift to a different field of activity.

Over the many years that I have worked with forecasts, I have noticed something strange. Every time a person close to me was destined to die, I became somehow distanced from that person. It seemed to start about eight to nine months before the moment of death. There may have been different reasons for this but any attempt at a reconciliation led to the opposite result and the relationship only worsened or broke down completely. It was just the same with Roman. We stopped communicating with each other about nine months before his death and, despite all my husband's efforts to change things, we did not pick up the connection. And when I spoke about this with Noel Thiel, a famous American astrologer, he said the same thing. Those people he knew whose time of death was approaching disappeared off his radar long beforehand. Many clairvoyants observe the same phenomenon. Perhaps those people who can influence a person's fate are deliberately cut off from a person who is destined to meet their death in the near future.

A strange incident occurred in my life recently. Two people I know came to me for a consultation and one of them, who was born under the sign of Scorpio, took up all the session leaving the other lady just ten minutes at the end. The second woman, an Aries, was very annoyed about it and said tensely that she would come the day after tomorrow when I might make time for her, too. She seemed anxious and her eyes sparkled feverishly. I was in a hurry to visit my mother in hospital and, for some reason, I too felt tense and could not look at her.

Once we were leaving and standing at the entrance to the building she kindly offered to give me a lift to the hospital. It would have been a great help and it was on her way but for some reason, I did not want to go with her. I felt a strange discomfort in her presence and wanted to leave as quickly as possible. I said that I would make my own way to the hospital and she left promising to call the following day.

A mere ten minutes later, the driver lost control of the vehicle and they both died in a collision. Her friend felt guilty afterwards for having taken up all my time during the session preventing the other woman and I from speaking. Evidently, the session would have been futile for the woman who died and it would not have changed anything. I don't even really remember what the deceased looked like so much as my powerful reluctance to get into the car with her.

Those who are at least a little versed in astrological symbolism will understand why a woman born under the sign of Scorpio received my consultation, while the Aries woman did not. Scorpio is the 8th sign for Aries, which symbolises death and destruction. Not only that, the Aries lady drove away in the Scorpio woman's car with her driver. This is not to say at all that any blame lay with the Scorpio woman. Her part in the situation was in a sense a kind of warning sign, along with the circumstance that immediately after the consultation, I was going to the hospital to visit my mother who had undergone a serious operation. The energy at this moment in time was heavy too, but understanding often only comes when it is too late.

Six months had passed since the day of Roman's death. It was summer, and my husband, my sister and I decided to mark what would have been his thirtieth birthday. The table was laid with a cake and cups of the Turkish coffee, which he loved and often drank in our office. We left a space at the table for him and one cup and a slice of cake were set out in his memory. And suddenly a faint, tender, barely perceptible sweet smell of either violets or decay swept past my face. We all exchanged looks — Roma was with us. The smell grew stronger and stronger until it felt like he had filled the room. He stayed with us for a while and then suddenly disappeared. After that, Roman stopped appearing in our dreams or making himself felt in other ways. He had completed his affairs on Earth and left.

BIRTH

Our office was situated opposite a maternity unit. I always considered this a positive location knowing that every hour, every minute a tiny person was being born opposite us. Doctors from the hospital often popped into our office and small astrology shop to buy books and newspapers. At that time, our shop was the only one like it selling mystical, occult and astrological literature.

One day, one of our regular customers, a 40-year-old neuropathologist, came in for a consultation. He was interested in astrology and had a good understanding of the basic principles. His wife was pregnant but could not give birth naturally — a month later she had a cesarean section. My acquaintance had three children but he was not happy about how they were developing as all three had problems with their health.

This time they were having a boy and my client had requested that we calculate the day and time of the Caesarean section. And although in theory I knew how this was done, in practice, I came up against a number of problems. I had a window of ten days, during which time the operation would have to be carried out. I chose two fortuitous days when the position of the planets was at its most harmonious. Then, I had to choose the better of those two. Both days were very good, but energetically speaking, they were also very different. A child born on the first day would be restrained, refined and intelligent, with a diplomatic, steady character, a fine sense of taste, and artistic gifts. A child born on the second of the two days would be sparkling, bold, charismatic, bright, restless, easily influenced, trusting and open. An individual's personality, potential and fate not only comes down to the day but the time of birth, too, but initially, the day is the most important thing. I met with the future father who thought long and hard and then chose the second day.

"The boy should be like that, at least, I would like to have a son like that."

The cesarean section was carried out on the appointed day and at the appointed time. The boy was strong and hardly ever ill; he was also cheerful and buoyant. We met last when the child was four years old, and, according to his father, he was developing much faster than his peers.

The theme of birth is one of the most mysterious and most captivating in the field of astrology and yet it is amazing how little we consider the fact that birth is the very first time a person comes into contact with the external world, and how little we do to make that first contact as painless and as comfortable as possible. We lavishly arrange the details of a funeral, a wedding and subsequent birthdays but we treat the appearance of a new life in this world relatively lightly.

The atmosphere in the average maternity unit not exactly evoke feelings of joy. They are usually full of dull-looking wards and irritable staff. If you're lucky, the midwife and doctor will be attentive and responsible at least. And if not, then the poor woman in labor has to adapt to the circumstances and, in general, cope with the pain, fear, doubt and suspense pretty much on her own. The father of the child is normally somewhere at a distance, the service staff often cannot be reached, and it feels like no-one could give two hoots about you or your child.

I realise that I am not painting a very optimistic picture of the average birth but it is one with which millions of women who have given birth will be familiar with. It is such a wild tradition, for example, to instantly take the child away from its mother. You would think it had been invented by the worst enemy of the entire human race! Meanwhile, everything related to pregnancy and childbirth has a direct impact on the fate of the child. Even the character of the physician observing the pregnancy and birth is significant.

I have two sons and my first pregnancy was observed by a beautiful, calm, confident woman. It was a difficult birth but she carried out her part in such a way that I never doubted for a moment that all would turn out well. My eldest son's life has not exactly been straightforward but he has wonderful qualities — he is efficient, very responsible, knows how to get along well with others and understands women perfectly. And, I should add, women show him the same in return. My eldest son is also very musical. He has the rare gift of perfect pitch and plays the guitar very well. It is unlikely that this is accidental as when I was pregnant, I was a first year student at the conservatory and played often. My son was born in the night and on the morning of that same day I had passed an exam and played the entire set program without incident.

My second pregnancy and the second birth were by comparison quick and easy. Unfortunately though, I gave birth on a shift being run by a tough woman who was domineering and rude. During the contractions, I began to moan loudly and without saying a word, she slapped me hard across the cheek. It was done with a careless movement, as if it were the only normal way to treat a woman in labor.

"No shouting here!" she said. It's the quiet hour and you'll wake everyone else up going on like that!" She had no idea how to assist at childbirth and tried to mask her ridiculous instructions by shouting that she had ended up with the stupid woman. Who knows how things would have ended it if had not been for an experienced, attentive midwife who decided to get involved. The midwife was the mother of one of my fellow students and she happened to recognise me. My tormentor was immediately removed from the scene, and after that the birth went easily and smoothly. I quickly gave birth to a wonderful boy and was completely over the moon.

My second son is very successful but he does not easily form romantic relationships. His girlfriends often seem in some vague manner to resemble the brash, eccentric woman from the hospital. However, I have no doubt that when he marries, his wife will have the kind and caring nature of my saviour midwife.

Having glimpsed a certain connection between the course of pregnancy, childbirth and the nature of the unborn child, I began to ask my friends, clients and acquaintances about their own experience and their answers confirmed my assumptions. Much of what happens to the mother during pregnancy and childbirth is subsequently manifest in the character of the baby.

So, once advising my good friend about her sons, I noted that the doctor who had observed her first pregnancy was no doubt a perfectionist. She was surprised by my comment but confirmed it to be true. Indeed, the individual in question was extremely careful and did not miss a single detail giving his patient instruction on the appropriate nutrition, sleep patterns, clothing, and therapeutic exercises. There is indeed something of this quality in her eldest son.

The doctor observing during her second pregnancy was the complete opposite — a very emotional and artistic person. He was interested in the sea, was a diver, and his relationship with the expectant mother developed in an unusual way. Their conversations were not so much focused on the mother and her unborn baby as on themes of the sea, relaxation, music and so on. And all this left an imprint on the character of her child. Today, he is a great artist, has a good feel for music, loves the sea and is generally a sensitive man, in touch with his emotions.

It is worth being very vigilant when taking medicines too and considering how essential they are to the mother and how they might affect the child's health. Where possible it is better to avoid pain killers, particularly those that cause drowsiness. The child 'pays' for the dulling effect afterwards with allergies and a susceptibility to alcohol and drugs.

The pain a woman experiences during childbirth is a sacred pain that a woman can tolerate. This is an integral part of the birth process in which each contraction brings you closer to the unborn baby. God truly only gives us tests that we are capable of enduring.

Pregnancy is one of the greatest mysteries of life. It represents the transition of the soul from one world to another, and is often preceded by dreams and other mystical events. The child of a friend of mine was in fact saved by a dream. Sensing that she was pregnant, she thought for a long time about whether to keep the child or have an abortion. Her marriage was going through a difficult period, and she decided not to keep the child. The night before the abortion was scheduled, she had an unusually vivid dream: she was walking down a long corridor and entered a large, brightly-lit room filled with rows of small cots with sleeping babies. A tall, beautiful woman in a white, luminous robe led her to the side of one of the cradles and showed her a wonderful baby with blond, wavy hair.

"This one is yours," she said softly and disappeared.

The next morning, my friend changed her mind about the abortion — she had firmly decided to give birth and she did indeed have a beautiful boy with wavy blond hair.

I was asked to calculate the time of a Caesarean section on many occasions and they always went well. Does this practice contradict religious concepts? To put it simply, 'is it a sin?' Apparently not, since we are only talking about those cases in which a woman cannot give birth naturally. In this case, either the astrologer chooses the moment for her or the doctor does. It is preferable that an astrologer choose when the procedure should be scheduled as they better understand the quality of a future moment in time. And if a person has turned to an astrologer in the first place, then their child is destined to be born that way. If a woman is able to give naturally, then the intervention of an astrologer is inappropriate and everything should be allowed to unfold as naturally as possible.

Even more complex and an even greater responsibility lies in choosing the moment for IVF treatment. In today's world this is a widespread procedure and many women who are unable to conceive naturally have successfully received IVF treatment. It has to be said that this is a very complex process, and often a successful result is not achieved straight away. I know women whose first attempts were unsuccessful and lived for years afterwards in anticipation of a miracle. Every attempt is a severe stress on the women's body. Moreover, there is the emotional stress when the treatment is unsuccessful and a women is suddenly thrown back into a state of hopelessness, insecurity and longing. The outcome can never be known beforehand and whether the treatment will be successful or not does not depend solely on the qualifications of the doctor in question. There are times when a woman's body simply cannot be open to accept a new life, and astrologers can tell when these periods in a women's life are occurring. They are linked to the phases of the Moon, retrograde planets and many other subtle astrological factors.

There is a reason why the great physicians of the past had a good knowledge of astrology and used it in the preparation of medicines and the treatment of their patients. Unfortunately, things have changed in this regard, which is of no credit to astrologers or physicians. The former because they have been unable to explain the value of astrological knowledge, and the latter because of their lack of openness, their dominant focus on material values and tendency to respond to advice from professionals in other fields as an invasion of their sacred territory.

Forgive me. It is not my intention to insult those doctors who selflessly struggle to combat disease and remain committed to their role despite the measly salary with which they are rewarded (in Russia at least). I am referring to the general trend in private, commercial medicine. By and large, this field operates as a profitable business and is aimed at wealthy segments of society.

What can a doctor working in this kind of system say to an astrologer who tells them that there are periods in which no-one should undergo IVF and that those periods can last up to 3-4 weeks? And there may be three to four periods like this over the course of a year. In addition, every woman's body has its own unique cycle including periods when implantation of the foetus will be unsuccessful and it is better to wait, sometimes for quite a long time.

And if fertilisation has occurred at a generally unfavourable time or a period in the individual's life that is not compatible, then the probability of a favourable outcome is minimal and instead of exhausting a woman's body with endless unsuccessful attempts, there is another option, which is to choose a fortuitous time and wait. Sometimes, this might involve waiting for as much as two to three years, sometimes less. A doctor who has no knowledge of astrology will never be able to choose a favourable time for IVF treatment. There is no other professional who can know the quality of a moment of time in the future like an astrologer can.

Typically, women turn to an astrologer in desperation after numerous unsuccessful attempts. Normally clients like this are hoping for a miracle and they can be quite challenging to work with. I advised a client once to wait six months. She found this suggestion very hard to accept desperate as she was by then for an imminent result.

"Why should I have to wait just because of the stars?"

I tried to explain to her that her own body was not yet ready to accept a child and that the situation in the family was such that this could not yet happen but it did not help. She spoke to a doctor and she had repeat IVF treatment two months later. This was her sixth or seventh attempt and it failed. After this incident, the woman rethought all sorts of things in her life. She became more patient, softer, and at the time proposed by an astrologer, a fertilised egg was implanted in her womb. And at the age of 46 she gave birth to two wonderful girls. Despite her age, her body coped brilliantly. She looked great both during the pregnancy and after giving birth and now she is a very happy mother. Her husband is also happy, although he did not believe in astrology or in the success of our joint venture. Now he has greater respect for all sorts of astrological recommendations and it was he who requested that I calculate the time and day of the Caesarean section. This must be the greatest reward for any astrologer, to see a happy family with healthy children. When I experience failure, I recall cases like this and the families I have been able to help and it makes me feel so much better.

Forecasting Mistakes

Sometimes clients ask, 'What is the probability of your forecasts coming true? Do you ever make mistakes?' Unfortunately, there is only one response I can give to that: 'Yes, I do.' It is not the astrology that is at fault, after all, we are talking about a perfectly harmonious predictive system. It is just that it is not always easy to comprehend.

Astrologers are human and like all other human beings, they sometimes make mistakes. And yet an astrologer errs at great cost involving vain hopes, ungrounded fears, and plans ineffectively made. Therefore, is it worth not 'charging into battle' until you have total confidence in yourself and have trained to the end both on the great figures of the past, whose lives are thoroughly documented, and on your friends who trust you and will share with you the events of their life in detail. The past is the best possible key to the future; in fact without understanding the past it is impossible to predict the future. Therefore, any consultation begins not with the future but with the past, and the astrologer must convey all sorts of information to the client: their main character traits, key events in their life and the purpose of the client's visit.

If an astrologer is for any reason unable to deduce this kind of information from the client's chart, then they should think twice before continuing to work with that person as the probability of error will be high.

A good practicing astrologer always has a group of regular clients, people who consult with them over a period of time and find the forecasts useful. There is a kind of compatibility between an astrologer and their regular clients that suggests both parties understand each other well. It is great if the astrologer's sun sign falls on the well aspected Jupiter and Venus placements in the client's chart. Jupiter and Venus are the planets of happiness and good luck, and so in this case, you can always expect positive results that make the communication between client and astrologer constructive and enjoyable.

All astrologers, clairvoyants, and fortune-tellers have their own 'Waterloo'. No-one can have a track record of one hundred percent accurate predictions; even the great Vanga sometimes erred.

My greatest defeat was related to the presidential elections. My political forecasts had been accurate for quite a long time, and this gave me a certain confidence that everything would work out just as well in the future. And when in a television program, I was asked who would be the next president, I cited the name of a person who could have become president but later unexpectedly withdrew from race. My forecast was based on the fact that only this candidate had stated in his speeches that the results of privatisation in Russia should be reviewed. The astrological forecast for the country was suggestive of a partial revision of the results of privatisation. The current president, on the contrary, quite categorically asserted the opposite — the results of privatisation would not be revised. However, when he was elected, he subsequently began to embark upon a different plan of action and now we are seeing the situation in Russia gradually change.

The results of a presidential election are extremely difficult to predict because in this context the country's horoscope is more important than the personality of the president. If a country is approaching a period of change that is inevitably accompanied by economic disaster, then the role of president will fall to an individual who is capable of bringing about these conditions.

For example, Boris Yeltsin, who was born under the sign of Aquarius was elected as president in what was a critical period for Russia. Aquarius is a symbol of freedom and anarchy; it is a sign that resists the principles of orderliness and structure. As pioneer, oppositionist and destroyer, Aquarius is unparalleled but would find it challenging to head any existing structure.

Therefore, Yeltsin stood out as an exceptional figure when he was in the camp of the opposition but once he became head of the country, he quickly lost his popularity. There was no one to fight and he amused himself by dismissing his government every three months or so.

But let us get back to the mistakes made by astrologers, clairvoyants and anyone who deals with the future. What should a forecaster do if they have made a prediction that does not match the unfolding of future events? It is probably best that the astrologer honestly admit the error, analyse the mistake and think over whatever system they are using.

It is slightly different with clairvoyants because they are not using complex calculations, they are simply seeing images of the future.

Sometimes clairvoyants see things clearly, vividly, and sometimes in encrypted, symbolic form.

A famous and very talented clairvoyant with whom I was acquainted once said that any potential future situation is subject to change, which explains why is might be seen in one way first and then another. She admits that she is not always able to predict the exact time a future event might take place and completely agrees that only the All-Highest can know everything. She very rarely gets things wrong, and if a prediction does prove inaccurate, she believes it is because that person is not supposed to receive certain information about the future, and so it is not given.

The reason why one person may know their future and another may not lies beyond the realm of human understanding. It is not something that can be explained, However, it is possible that behind the 'errors' forecasters make, there may lie a complex plan that shapes the future much more effectively than an accurate forecast would.

Once, a friend of mine, a very dynamic and charming lady, turned to me with the eternal female question — would she marry the man she was currently seeing. And although it was evident that men of his type rarely divorce their wives and that this woman's marriage to him could only officially take place in a very distant future, for some reason, I said, 'Yes, he loves you and he may well marry you.'

This friend later consulted someone else for a reading who gave her the opposite information. His precise words were, 'don't waste your time on him... he'll never marry you.'

The romance continued, however, and the man in question helped my friend in all sorts of ways. No marriage between them had yet taken place and then my friend started to wonder whether she really wanted the relationship after all at the same time as acknowledging the positive role he had played in her fate.

When I did her forecast, I was absolutely sure that in her case, it was not marriage that was essential, so much as the love and support that had made her life happier and more stable. Not least because for the next four years it was clear that no-one else more suitable was going to appear on the horizon. My words reflected the situation at that moment in time and maybe this was more important than an accurate forecast for the future.

Although situations such as this one are very rare, it does make you stop and think about whether a person can always know the truth in every circumstance. Indeed, the most important principle for any astrologer is 'do no harm'.

THE OTHER SIDE OF VICTORY

No-one likes having to wait, not for a new love, a new job, a lucky streak or even, let's face it, a bus. Waiting is a painful, anxious state associated with the unknown, uncertainty and fear of the future. At least once in their life, everyone finds themselves in a position where the old has been wiped away and the new has not arrived yet, and they have no idea when things will start to change. Imagine for example a person has lost their job. In the past lie intrigue, struggle, conflicts and stress. It might have been a difficult time but at least it was a life in which there were desires, hopes and you could take action. Now all that has suddenly come to an end and there is nothing to replace it, no struggle, no intrigue, no hopes and no work. Friends and colleagues gradually distance themselves all busy with their own lives. There is no suitable work available and wherever that person turns, they receive a polite refusal. Someone promises to help but it is all so vague, foggy and stretched out over time. Gradually emptiness sets in and then come the hardest part — the waiting, which might last a month, a year, or even several years.

Another example is when the person you love walks out on you and you realise they are gone for good. First there was the hope of saving the relationship. That was followed by despair, hatred and suffering, and then, in a single moment, it is all over — gone. Ahead lies loneliness and uncertainty.

The state of waiting and expectation that a person experiences when they are between two distinct periods in their life can last for ages or it might come down to a matter of minutes.   So it is for example for a sportsman, who is about to head out into the arena, or an actor about to begin a performance, a pianist about to give a concert, or an orator about to give a speech. Anyone who has ever experienced this state will remember it well and knows that the hardest thing is not the performance — it is what you have to go through beforehand in anticipation of the performance.

There is truth in the saying that waiting for death is worse than death itself. By this time, you have moved away from your colleagues, fans, and loved ones and you stand alone for a while before going out to face the public. How you spend this time, whether you will be able to focus and prepare for the 'leap' bringing to the public everything that you have worked for, will depend on these few short moments. You can panic, lose yourself and everything that you so want to convey to people, or you can pull it all together, concentrate and mentally run through the future performance attuning yourself to victory. It is in these moments that a person either wins the battle or loses.

It is the same in longer periods of waiting; how the next active period in a person's life will play out depends on how they have spent the quieter times. Life is like a chunk of zebra: every black stripe is always followed by a lighter one. The times when you are alone, abandoned and seemingly not needed by anyone are so much more important than the times when you are in demand and everyone loves you and needs you. No-one wants the grey chrysalis until it becomes a bright, beautiful butterfly. And still, there would be no butterfly if it were not for the chrysalis!

The ability to pull oneself together at the right moment, not cave in or panic is the most valuable quality that distinguishes successful individuals from others who are less successful.

People we think of as being successful experience periods of stagnation and stress and times when they feel unwanted just like anyone else. The difference is how effectively they use that time! You only have to remember the periods of exile and solitude in Pushkin's life such as when he was quarantined at Mikhailovskoe, and the famous 'Boldin Autumn[9],' or the no less well-known example of Nikolai Ostrovsky[10] and his novel 'How The Steel Was Tempered'. Even the fictional hero Dumas Count of Monte Cristo changed having spent 20 years in prison. Despite how different all these figures might be, one thing unites them: after periods of forced isolation, they went through a transformation and reemerged into society' in a completely different capacity. They looked after themselves, worked and above all, simply got on with living life, doing whatever the time required of them. They did not cling to the past but focused on the future, consciously and unconsciously. They saw their own, special meaning in these forced periods of loneliness and made the most of the time they had.

To see meaning in what is happening and to relate consciously to the events in one's life, no matter how negative they may seem, is the

---

[9] The most fruitful period in the life of the great Russian poet Alexander Pushkin

[10] Famous Russian socialist realist writer best known for his novel "How the Steel Was Tempered", which he wrote undaunted by blindness and immobility caused by his declining health.

main step towards future success. However various negative situations in life might differ, the one thing they have in common is this: the reason you are not in demand in because you are not needed the way you are. You are being called to change and if you resist the process, the emptiness that surrounds you will only grow.

Such is the law of the universe — a person only becomes isolated, when they need to be alone. According to the principle of synchronism* coined by C. G. Jung ** our existence is full of hidden meaning, on account of which we find ourselves in circumstances that correspond to the state of our psyche. So, you can curse at an unfair boss or former lover and blame them for everything that has ever happened to you but then you will live only in your memories, become depressed, lose interest in life and completely drive yourself into a corner.

Periods of emptiness and quiet are valuable because they give you the freedom to act. At times like this, a person is free of their former obligations. What a great opportunity to do something new! And yet freedom is not for everyone. We are used to a rigidly structured life in which our daily schedule is dictated by work and family responsibilities. But when there is none of that to distract us, a person can be left to their own devices. The question is whether they will have the strength and courage to build their own path in life, to focus on themselves and not waste time moaning about life.

Never reproach yourself for the mistakes you might have made. Never allow yourself to get trapped living in the past. Prepare for the future. It is only by aspiring to the future and holding to the belief that someday, all that you are doing now will be valued, that these difficult periods can be lived more easily and acquire meaning. For as Nietzsche wrote, 'He who has a why to live can bear almost any how.' And another sage once said, 'Give me a place to stand on, and I will move the Earth'. Periods in which everyone seems to have forgotten about you can be that very same place to stand on from which you can turn your life around. All you have to do is learn to navigate it.

Tatiana Borsch

* Astrology is built on the principle of synchronism. According to Jung, events that do not have a causal relationship, but have a similar meaning - at the symbolic level, manifest themselves simultaneously.

** Carl Gustav Jung (1875-1961) - Swiss psychologist and psychiatrist, founder of analytical psychology. Claimed that he considered astrology to be the progenitor of modern scientific psychology. Formulated the principle of synchronism.